The Rich Get Richer
The growth of inequality in Britain in the 1980s

JOHN RENTOUL

London
UNWIN PAPERBACKS
Boston   Sydney

First published in paperback by Unwin® Paperbacks,
an imprint of Unwin Hyman Limited in 1987

UNWIN HYMAN LIMITED
Denmark House
37-39 Queen Elizabeth Street
LONDON SE1 2QB
and
40 Museum Street, LONDON WC1A 1LU

Allen & Unwin Australia Pty Ltd
8 Napier Street, North Sydney, NSW 2060, Australia

Unwin Paperbacks with Port Nicholson Press
60 Cambridge Terrace, Wellington, New Zealand

British Library Cataloguing in Publication Data
Rentoul, John
  The rich get richer : the growth of
  inequality in Britain in the eighties.
  1. Equality 2. Social Classes—Great
  Britain—History—20th century
  3. Great Britain—Social conditions
  —1945-
  1. Title
  305'.0941   HN385.5
  ISBN 0 04 440099 3

Set in 10 on 12 point Garamond ITC
Printed and bound in Great Britain by
Billings & Sons Ltd, London and Worcester

John Rentoul has worked on the *New Statesman* as a reporter since 1983. In the guise of the Politics of Envy Unit he monitors top pay and perks. Before that he was a journalist on *Accountancy Age*. He contributed "The Case Against" to *Privatisation*, a Papermac election special edited by Julia Neuberger, in May 1987. Mrs Thatcher has been Prime Minister for most of his adult life.

ACKNOWLEDGEMENTS

Many thanks to Richard Kuper; John Mullan; Anne McDermid; Anthony Barnett; the *New Statesman* staff, especially Andrew Lumsden, Sarah Benton, Vicky Hutchings and John Lloyd; and Bernard Gottlieb.

CONTENTS

PART I:
WHAT HAS HAPPENED

1. INTRODUCTION

"Straw hat, £230, by Patricia Underwood,
Browns, 27 South Molton St, London W1"
— *Harpers and Queen*, July 1986.

"It's a neater, cleaner spring and summer: dress for cocktails, weddings and Ascot in simple, no-fuss glamour." For example: cream and black spotted silk dress, £866. Black speckled rayon mix jacket and matching black and white patterned viscose skirt, £695. For men, black and blue cotton knit V-neck jumper, about £250, with navy, black and white striped linen jacket, about £350 (*Harpers and Queen*, April 1986).

Black crocodile stamped belt with silver conch shells, £5,550. And, of course, that hat. Who's wearing it?

The *Tatler* in July/August 1986 featured three newly-wed "girls", all aligned politically with Wages for Housework *up to a point* (they believe giving dinner parties is a full-time and worthwhile job) and all passionately keen on *shopping*.

Olivia Wentworth Rump, now Mrs Fackelmayer, wife of German-born Friedel, who works for an American bank in London:

> I have no interest in working. I feel quite confident that I don't have to justify my life — there's always masses to do and never enough time in the day. I've learnt to really enjoy cooking. About once a fortnight we have a dinner party for twelve or fourteen of our really good friends. More often six or eight of us will have supper in the kitchen, and occasionally we splurge and buy a huge tin of caviar and eat it in front of the fire with a couple of friends. We're very big on Sunday lunches with masses of people — twenty friends and children. About once every six weeks we entertain more formally — when we don't know the people so well or if it's business. Then I get a cook and a couple of waitresses in. In an average week we'll go to a dinner party and out to a restaurant with friends once or twice.

Tricia — not one of the *Tatler*'s newly-weds — is a less enthusiastic eater than Olivia. She is a single mother living on social security, quoted in the book of London Weekend Television's series on poverty, *Breadline Britain*:

> I don't think I could eat every day if people put it in front of me. It's just what I've got used to, the way I've got used to living because you are limited to what you can spend and you get into that way of life. [1]

Tatler Case Study Number Two Emma Muspratt — who married "a headhunter" three years ago — recognises that "I'm very lucky in that I don't have to work," although she does some typing at home. "At the moment I transcribe tapes for a journalist writing a book on people and their attitudes to work. It's fascinating and educational and it's very useful to have a knowledge of what people do." She gives one or two dinner parties a week ("I love entertaining"), goes to dinner parties twice a week and goes on holidays. "Last year we were out of the country one weekend a month."

Welcome to the twelve-holiday-a-year family. On the other hand, the fascinating and educational *Breadline Britain* survey found that in 1983 there were 13 million people in Britain who couldn't afford to go on holiday at all.

Case Study Number Three, shipping heiress Verena, married Canadian banking and beer heir Ian Molson in April 1986:

> I love giving dinner parties but we don't entertain here because we don't have a dining room. That's a reason for moving. We give dinner parties in the country when we have people to stay for the weekend — we've got a little house in Hertfordshire on the estate at home which my father gave us. My life has changed dramatically since marriage. I love being loved. Money means nothing — it's emotional security that's important. We love going on holiday together. It's just utter bliss to be together. We ski as much as possible — it's a wonderful way to relax.

Breadline Britain quotes Anne, mother of three children in inner Birmingham, whose husband has been on short-time working for three years, and who is not so sure that money means nothing:

> When we all go out we walk. We walk a lot. It's very rare we use buses. The cost of coaches, the trains, they're all expensive. I think it's important for kids to get out of the city so they can see things

they probably wouldn't see otherwise, like wild flowers. But it's just impossible.

For Verena Molson transport is a matter of taste.

One interest we don't share is my passion for cars. I *love* speed. I drive a BMW 318i. Ian's got a BMW 323i with every extra you can think of, but he just wants a car to get from A to B. I have an absolute craving for a Porsche 911. I spend a lot of time shopping for clothes. I adore clothes. I love shopping for them and I love putting them together. I'd never go off and spend hundreds of pounds on one fantastic dress ... unless it's something very special, then I will. I think one must remember the whole time that one's only here on loan and we do have a motto: enjoy each day to the full. We always try to do what we want to do. We're very fortunate, we really are.

Of course, nobody wants to make the less fortunate feel awkward. As Olivia Fackelmayer says:

I don't want anyone to feel they're on parade and must dress up when they come to dinner. I love clothes, but I wouldn't judge someone by what they're wearing; when they walk into a room you just notice whether they look nice or not. Funnily enough I worry less about my appearance since I've been married. As a single girl going out every night it was very important not to wear the same thing twice.

(According to *Breadline Britain*, some people have serious difficulty wearing the same thing once, like the 4.5 million people who can't afford a warm waterproof coat.)

Now I'm more relaxed, but I've always had a lot of clothes. They tend to be expensive, but that's a coincidence. My taste is classical but I love to overdo it when we go out. When I get bored of my clothes I give them away. I've got a very willing nanny, and of course dailies and friends. I buy lots and lots of shoes. I have a passion for them.

Other people, of course, have a need for them, especially children. Sandra (interviewed in *Breadline Britain*) refuses to buy second-hand shoes for her three children, whom she has to bring up on the low wages her husband brings home.

It's all right in summer but in the cold weather you get to school and they say you mustn't keep those damp shoes on. You've got to take two pairs of shoes. Sometimes you can't afford two bloody pairs of shoes. And you can't put the children into them plimsolls. They say don't bring those things in, they're bad for their feet.[2]

This book is an attempt to describe and explain the enrichment of the few since 1979. It's a commonplace that the rich have got richer under Mrs Thatcher and that the poor have got poorer. But is it true? If so, why has it happened? Who are the beneficiaries? And how rich is rich? Part I examines the gap between rich and poor in Britain today, and how it has widened since 1979. It looks at why it has widened when there's a consensus that the gap was already too great. Part II tries to set out what can be done about it, and examines the obstacles to doing it. It looks at why people think Britain ought to be more equal, and yet are resigned to great inequality continuing.

Anxiety about a divided Britain appears to be widespread, but perhaps it doesn't run very deep. Maybe people are uncertain about how unequal society is, and see divisions as geographic or cultural rather than as imposed by material inequality on citizens of the same society. The allegation that Britain is divided into "Two Nations", growing further apart under a government dedicated to the interests of one over the other, incites fatalism, especially among people who aren't quite sure which Nation they're supposed to be in.

Three Nations
But there are now Three Nations, not Two, and the Thatcher government has pampered not just the rich but even more that other, discreet Nation, the super rich. The Three Nations are the *haves*, the *have nots* and the *have lots*. And, although it has become more acceptable to do so, the *have lots* try not to flaunt their wealth for fear of drawing attention to their enrichment behind what is advertised as wider home and share ownership.

"Two Nations", since its coinage by Benjamin Disraeli in 1845, has been a weapon for Tory wets against ruling-class-consciousness of the kind now exemplified by Norman Tebbit. But Two Nations is not an adequate term to describe the divisiveness of Thatcherism. Two Nation rhetoric, whether coded Wetspeak, Alliance flannel or full-blooded class hatred, hides the extent of the changes in British society since about 1979. A simple division of the country into rich and poor implies that improving the lot of the poor has to be at the expense of the modestly well-off: if you give to one nation you have to take from the other. It also implies that there's a continuity of interests between the middle class and the very rich, which, up to a point, is true. The very rich have co-opted parts of the middle class — private education for instance is not restricted to the fabulously rich (6.6 per cent of all children are at private schools). They share a common interest in the ownership of property and the performance of the Stock Exchange. But the very rich do live in a different world, one marked out by the scale of their capital.

Not since the 1920s has it been possible to talk of a leisured class, but the forces of reaction are now reassembling an élite who own enough capital to live on. At 1987 rates of interest and — crucially — 1987 tax rates, a person needs £162,000-worth of capital (in addition to their home) to secure an income equivalent to average earnings, and to maintain the value of their capital against inflation. There are now at least 280,000 of such potentially-idle rich individuals in Britain,[3] and what's more, since the abolition of tax on lifetime capital transfers, they can pass on their wealth untouched by the tax person's hands, for generation after generation. Or, as Mrs Thatcher put it in April 1986, their wealth holdings will "topple like a cascade down the line of the family".

These are the real beneficiaries of the Thatcher enrichment. Every tax relief or state asset sold at a discount to sweeten the middling sort of voter is worth a large multiple to the super-rich. The abolition of unearned income surcharge in 1984, worth a few pounds a year to Mr and Mrs Comfortably Retired of Eastbourne on their Lonrho dividends, was worth over £1 million every year to "Tiny" Rowland, chair and chief executive of same. The flotation of British Telecom in 1984, worth £200 to anyone enterprising enough to fill in a form and lucky enough to have or borrow £250, was worth £88,000 to chairperson Sir George Jefferson, whose pay doubled in two years to £172,206 a year. In each case there are the silent masses of people who cannot afford Tory giveaways at all; they are only given to them that hath. The accumulation of wealth proceeds as silently and as unobtrusively as the degradation of the poor, worn down by long-term unemployment.

That's the impressionistic view. But what is really going on? What do the cold statistics reveal about the extent and growth of inequality since May 1979?

---

1. Joanna Mack and Stewart Lansley, *Poor Britain*, George Allen and Unwin

1985, p. 95. Publishing details of all books mentioned in the text are given in the Bibliography on p. 185.

2. *Poor Britain*, p. 150.

3. Sum based on median earnings (adults in full-time employment) in April 1986 of £8,518 a year (New Earnings Survey), updated to April 1987 by average earnings, to £9,156, less 11 per cent average housing costs (Family Expenditure Survey 1984: "The Effects of Taxes and Benefits on Household Income 1984", *Economic Trends*, July 1986), which comes to £8,118. To produce this income and preserve the real value of wealth would require assets of £162,000 assuming interest rates of around 10 per cent with inflation at 5 per cent. The estimate of the number of rich individuals worth £270,000 in 1987, 280,000, the richest 0.6-0.7 per cent of adults, is based on Inland Revenue estimates of the distribution of wealth in the UK, 1983, *Inland Revenue Statistics 1985*, as projected to 1986 by Professor Shorrocks of Essex University, and updated to 1987 by 10 per cent. Typically, an individual worth £270,000 would be one of a couple worth £324,000 plus a house worth £216,000; property typically accounts for 40 per cent of individuals' total wealth.

2. THE SHAPE OF INEQUALITY

"Why are the many poor?" — title of Fabian
Society pamphlets 1 (1884) and 500 (1984).

What has happened to the distribution of income and wealth under
the Conservatives? The slightly surprising answer is that although
inequality of income has increased sharply since 1979, inequality of
wealth appears not to have changed. But first, to look at the history
of redistribution in this century.

Taking income, including that from investments, first, the top 1
per cent's share halved between the Second World War and 1979.
The share of the next 9 per cent of the population stayed the same,
while the rest of the top half gained. Much of this shift took place
before 1955, since when changes have been gradual, until 1979. By
then, Britain had one of the more equal distributions of income in
the world. In the 1970s, only Sweden and Australia had more equal
incomes out of a group of nine countries, the others being the United
States, Canada, France, Japan, West Germany and Ireland.[1]

As for the distribution of wealth, a more marked trend towards
greater equality was apparent for most of this century. The share of
personal wealth owned by the top 1 per cent of adults fell from about
three-fifths in the 1920s to one-fifth by 1979. The proportion owned
by the next 4 per cent stayed at about another fifth, while the rest of
the top half steadily increased its share from about one-fifth to three-
fifths, leaving the bottom half of the population where they started
— with virtually nothing.

Since 1979, in income terms, there has been a sharp increase in the
share of the top 10 per cent, with the top 1 per cent gaining most, to
recover the (after-tax) share it had in the 1960s. The share of the next
9 per cent hasn't been so high since the war. The Top People's gain
has been at the expense (at least initially) of the share of the middle
third and, most damagingly, that of the bottom 10 per cent of the
population. In just the first four years of the Thatcher government,
the income of the top 10 per cent of the population, after tax, rose
from six and a half times that of the bottom 10 per cent to seven and
a half times.[2] I estimate that income in Britain is now distributed as
unequally as that in the United States, which has one of the more
unequal distributions of income among industrialised countries.

The trend towards more equal distribution of wealth among the top half of the population, however, was only halted in 1979 — not reversed. The latest figures are for 1984, and show no change in shares over the period. But because the value of total personal wealth has increased quite sharply since 1979, while the rich have maintained the same very large proportional share, they have got very much richer in money terms without increasing their percentage share of the total. Only half the population owns significant amounts of wealth — the poorer half still owns a mere one-fourteenth of the total — and even among the richer half wealth is much more concentrated than income. Wealth was distributed more unequally in Britain than in the United States, Canada, Australia and New Zealand until the 1970s. However, the steady trend throughout the first seven decades of this century towards a more equal distribution — among the richer half of the population — means that the pattern is now similar to that in these countries, the only ones with which meaningful comparisons can be made. [3]

These descriptions of inequality are deliberately simplified to bring out the trends, describing proportions — rather than amounts — attributed to percentages of the population or adults in rank order. There are of course many other ways to describe inequality. We could compare the standard of living in money terms of different groups instead of the abstract differential between them, or their share of a total. Instead of dividing an imaginary ranking up into percentages, we could look at the fate and composition of actual social groups, such as the unemployed, pensioners, nurses or the "ruling class". Or we could compare families and households rather than individuals, to take account of different needs.

We could produce numerical comparisons, such as that the top 1 per cent own three times as much wealth as the bottom half of the population, or that 3,100 people earned over £500 an hour in 1985. [4] While such comparisons can be composed *ad nauseam*, they only have a momentary effect, by putting together things that are not usually seen side by side. People normally have rather limited horizons, comparing their income with people in similar jobs and their wealth with their social peer group. The very poor or the very rich exist in "different worlds" with which comparisons cease to have much meaning, unless they can be stated in new "same world" terms and we can briefly goggle at the noughts. They don't shed much light on the complicated social texture of unequal resources, circumstances and relationships that separate extremes, extremes which seem insupportable when compared out of context. The way in which that "context" supports extreme inequalities and obstructs change is the subject of Part II.

Different Ways of Being Unequal

There are also many different ways in which a given quantity of resources can be divided up unequally. If you divide £5 between three people thus, £3, £1 and £1, is that more unequal than £2, £2 and £1? (Only if you give yourself the £3.) Or take three people earning £7,000, £9,000 and £20,000 a year. After the Revolution, the same amount of pay could be distributed equally, £12,000 each.

Or, to avert the erection of the barricades, the richest one could buy off the middle one, by transferring £4,000 to her, to give £7,000, £13,000 and £16,000. The middle one is better off than if she throws in her lot with the lower orders, and the richest one loses less. This is the "greed principle", which, although it never operates as explicitly as that, underpins the unequal distribution of income. The gap between richest and poorest may have become narrower, but the person on £7,000 is no better off. If that's equality, grumbles the proletariat, they can keep it.

Or what if the person on £20,000 were the benevolent employer of the other two and agreed to pay them both £8,000 to demonstrate her commitment to the principle of equal pay? Liberal philosopher John Rawls would think that this was more just, because he judges societies by the position of the "least advantaged". But is it more *equal*?

There is a purely mathematical measure of how equal a distribution of numbers is, called the Gini coefficient. It ignores entirely the problem of distribution shape. A Gini coefficient of 0 per cent means a completely equal distribution (£12,000 each); 100 per cent means a completely unequal distribution (one has £36,000, the other two have nothing). But, in between, the Gini coefficient comes to more or less the conclusions you'd expect a mathematical formula to come to. These are the Gini scores for the imaginary situations above:

£7,000, £9,000 and £20,000 — 24%
£7,000, £13,000 and £16,000 — 17%
£8,000, £8,000 and £20,000 — 22%

The score for all disposable incomes in Britain in 1983 was 31 per cent, up from 28 per cent in 1977.[5] The score for the distribution of wealth was 68 per cent in 1984 — unchanged since 1979.

Perhaps as important as the Fabians' century-old question is "why are the few rich?" It seems to be true of all societies that there are lots of poor people and few rich; in other words, if you put incomes or wealth holdings in order of size, the middle one (called the median in statistical jargon) is always smaller than the average (all of them added together and divided by the number of earners or wealth-holders, known in statistical terms as the mean). In this case the person earning £9,000 (the median) gets less than the average, which is £12,000. In Britain in 1985, median full-time male earnings were £8,986, whereas the average was £9,984, a thousand pounds more. In real life, we tend to have $3-1-1$ shaped inequality rather than $2-2-1$, though it is more applicable to the top than to the bottom. The bottom half of British earnings has a touch of the $2-2-1$s about it, in that wages seem to cluster closer together below the median, before plunging quite quickly towards the bottom end of the scale.

At the top, the shape of inequality is so regular that there is a geometric formula called the Pareto curve which can predict how steeply incomes and wealth holdings rise as you go higher up the scale. For instance, in 1985/86 the Inland Revenue estimates that 7,000 single people or married couples earned over £100,000. Halve the amount to £50,000 and the number of incomes above it multiplies sevenfold to 52,000. Reduce the threshold to £20,000 and the number of incomes above it exceeds a million. Similarly with wealth: in 1986 there were about 20,000 individuals worth over £1 million, and only 435,000 worth over £190,000; but reduce the threshold to £75,000 and there are over 2 million people above it.

The shape of inequality matters because it has moral and practical consequences. If large disparities between rich and poor are a bad thing and should be reduced, then the rich are going to be clobbered harder in a $3-1-1$ shaped distribution than a $2-2-1$ shaped one. Conservatives use the fact that societies have $3-1-1$ shaped inequality to argue that there aren't very many rich people and so it isn't worth taxing them more heavily — the "Not Enough Rich People" canard. The point about very highly concentrated income or wealth is that although there are fewer people above the average than below it, they are further above it, and therefore have a greater ability to pay taxes.

Unfortunately the evidence on the combined inequalities of income and wealth, although this is clearly very important, is very partial. If none of the top 1 per cent of wealth holders (who own 20 per cent of all personal wealth in Britain) were, say, in Neil Kinnock's top "four or five per cent" of earners, this would have profound implications for Labour's taxation policy. Although people with high incomes tend also to be the top wealth-owners, this need not necessarily be the case. There is, for example, a substantial minority of retired people who have fairly low incomes and high wealth — and others who have high incomes and almost no savings.

The Inland Revenue's Survey of Personal Incomes (1983/84) records no one who lives on investment income alone (excluding pensions), meaning that a statistically insignificant number of people live solely on income from their wealth. It also shows that over 90 per cent of the 221,000 couples and single people with total income over £30,000 a year had some investment income, and that the average amount rose sharply with total income, of which it constituted only 5 per cent. Which suggests that top earners tend overwhelmingly to be top wealth owners, but doesn't prove it conclusively, or give us much idea of the precise nature of the correlation.

---

1. The Royal Commission on the Distribution of Income and Wealth, *Report No 5* (Cmnd. 6999), HMSO 1977; Chapter 6, "International comparisons of the distribution of personal incomes". The comparison the Royal Commission felt was most reliable was on the basis of the incomes of families, or in statistical language "consumer units", which is a cross between the British households and tax units (meaning related people living in the same household, or single people). This information was only available for the UK, United States and Canada. In 1975 the UK had a more equal distribution than the United States, with Canada somewhere in between. But the differences were not that great. The top fifth of units in the UK had 40 per cent of pre-tax income; in Canada the figure was 44 per cent and in the United States, 46 per cent. The bottom two-fifths in the UK had 17 per cent (in Canada, 14 per cent, and in the United States, 13.5 per cent). The Royal Commission also produced one comparison of after-tax income inequality, in the UK, West Germany and Sweden, on the basis of households in the early 1970s. In 1972 the top fifth of households had 38 per cent of after-tax income in the UK, 37 per cent in Sweden and markedly more, 45 per cent, in West Germany in 1970 and 1975 (1972 figure not available).

2. Central Statistical Office Blue Book series 1949 to 1981/82; continuation of burgeoning share of top 10 per cent confirmed by New Earnings Survey data to 1986 (top quarter of the New Earnings Survey is approximately

equivalent to top 10 per cent of all adults). The ratios between top and bottom tenths is for "equivalent incomes" of the whole population including children derived from Family Expenditure Surveys by Nick Morris and Ian Preston, "Taxes, Benefits and the Distribution of Income 1968 – 83", *Fiscal Studies*, November 1986 (see pp. 26 – 7).

3. Again, the Royal Commission is the only recent source of thorough analysis. It published a background paper called *The Distribution of Wealth in Ten Countries* in 1979 (see Bibliography on p. 185). Despite its title, the paper's author, Alan Harrison, was only able to make meaningful comparisons between Britain and the United States, and to a lesser extent Canada and Ireland. He refused to offer a "league table" of countries. "To do so would be to prompt many interpretations for which we would not wish to be responsible." He is very rude about even the Australian and New Zealand estimates, which are also based on death duty information (all other countries only have unreliable survey evidence, see p. 42). The crude evidence he presents suggests that wealth in Australia and New Zealand is more equally distributed than in Britain. If we are less scrupulous than Harrison we might accept surveys as evidence of trends if not actual inequalities. In Sweden, for all we know, wealth may be distributed as unequally as in Britain or the United States: the richest 1 per cent of *households* is reported as owning about a fifth of all personal wealth (Spant, forthcoming, cited by Professor Edward Wolff in "Estimates of Household Wealth Inequality in the United States, 1962 – 83", unpublished paper, New York University, May 1986). The distribution among individual adults would be more equal, although under-reporting would make the distribution seem more equal than it really is. But the historical trend is similar to Britain's: the share of the richest 1 per cent declined almost continuously from 50 per cent in 1920 to 20 per cent in 1975. Between 1975 and 1983, however, the share of the richest 1 per cent has stayed the same.

4. Assuming a forty-hour week and fifty-week year. The Inland Revenue's projection (Hansard, 21 May 1985) from the 1982/83 Survey of Personal Incomes, that 7,000 tax units earned over £100,000 in 1985/86 (that is, excluding investment income) implies at least 3,100 individuals with earnings over this level if the tax units are broken down into single people and couples in the same ratio as all those with total income over £30,000 in 1982/83, which is the only category available for comparison.

5. This is the score for the distribution of "equivalent income" among the whole population (see Note 2). This means that the score is not strictly comparable with that for wealth, although the distribution of income among adults on the same basis as the wealth estimates would probably give an even lower Gini score.

3. INEQUALITY OF INCOMES

Between Rich and Poor

"Most of our people have never had it so good."
— Prime Minister Harold Macmillan, July 1957.
"We've never had it so good for the 87 per cent
of us who are working." — Employment
Minister Lord Young, May 1986.

Eighty-seven per cent? There are about 38 million people of working age, of whom about 24 million, or 60 per cent, are in work. Who are the 14 million who don't have jobs? Well, in round numbers, 3.2 million are officially unemployed, 5.7 million married women aren't working and aren't entitled to supplementary benefit, 2.3 million men and unmarried women are "keeping house", permanently unable to work or are otherwise inactive, 1.5 million are pupils or full-time students and 0.4 million are on government job and training schemes. How well off they are depends either on the wage of the person they live with, or on student grants or social security benefits, although the increase in unemployment, training schemes and the fact that many married women might want to work but now can't means that around three million are worse off now than they would be if unemployment were at the same level as in 1979.

Include the ten million retired people and Lord Young's 87 per cent who've allegedly never had it so good are only 49 per cent of the adult population. And so how good are these 87 per cent (that are really a minority of the electorate) having it?

Statistics, Damned Statistics and Lies
First let's look at the earned income of people in work. There are two main sources of information about the distribution of earnings: the Inland Revenue's Survey of Personal Incomes, based on a sample of tax returns, is used for forecasting future tax revenue. The figures are published thirty-two months after the end of the tax year in question, although some Inland Revenue projections to the current tax year are published in ministerial answers to parliamentary questions. The Department of Employment's New Earnings

Survey, in April each year, is the biggest pay survey in Britain, covering around 110,000 employees, one in every hundred on PAYE (the Pay-As-You-Earn tax collection system). It provides figures for individuals rather than "tax units", that is, single people and married couples treated as one unit.

There are two other sources of survey material: the Family Expenditure Survey (FES), contains detailed information about household and family income and spending based on a fairly small sample of interviews (7,000 households containing 20,000 people), and the Labour Force Survey, which produces information on the extent of part-time work, self-employment and second jobs. The FES is the main source of information on the distribution of social security benefit income.

Now you would have thought, and not just because Lord Young says so, that the vast majority of those in work are better off now than they were in 1979. (Certainly, another series of statistics produced by the Central Statistical Office, the figure for "personal disposable income per head", rose by 11 per cent after taking inflation into account, between 1979 and 1986.)[1] This is not so. Although the data to give a definitive answer are simply not available, it is quite likely that getting on for *one-third* of those *in work* have lost the battle with inflation that Margaret Thatcher thinks they've won since 1979.

This isn't immediately obvious from a casual glance at the statistics. But first, to some of the ambiguities involved in sweeping assertions of Lord Young's kind. When he says we are better off than in 1979, he doesn't mean that as individuals we have increased our incomes by more than inflation. Some people working now were at school in 1979 and are obviously "better off" in income terms, while others who were working in 1979 have retired and are "worse off" on their pensions. When we talk of losers and gainers, we have to treat categories of people over time, rather than to try to sum up the experience of individuals. The simplest way of doing this is to put everyone in rank order and to compare, say, the bottom fifth or the top 1 per cent.

But not only is Lord Young's 87 per cent really a minority of the adult population, it also fragments as soon as it's examined. Only two-thirds of the 87 per cent are full-time employees (one-fifth are part-timers, one-tenth are full-time self-employed). These are the 16 million people covered by the New Earnings Survey.

A casual glance at the New Earnings Survey figures (see Table 1)

TABLE 1

Distribution of Earned Income 1979 – 1986

Annual pay	1979 (adjusted to 1986 money)	1986
10% earned more than	£12,642	£15,194
25% earned more than	£9,924	£11,471
50% earned more than	£7,741	£8,518
25% earned less than	£5,912	£6,282
10% earned less than	£4,717	£4,888

Full-time adult employees, gross earnings in constant 1986 prices, Great Britain only.

Source: New Earnings Survey, Department of Employment. 1979 figures are author's calculations from figures for men and women separately.[2]

would suggest that Lord Young is right. From the inflation-adjusted figures, it could look as if everyone in full-time work saw their pay go up in real terms, although the higher up the pay scale you are, the bigger the rise. But the figures contain a statistical illusion. In 1979 there were 19 million full-time employees; in 1986 there were only 16 million. Almost all of the 16 million in 1986 may have been earning more than almost all the 19 million in 1979; but suppose you were the lowest-paid employee in Britain in 1986: you would come 16 millionth if all employees were put in order of earnings, and probably earn less than £4,000 a year. Whoever was 16 millionth in 1979 would have been 3 million places up from the bottom, which is somewhere between the bottom 25 per cent and the bottom 10 per cent, earning over £5,000.[3]

We need to look at numbers, not proportions, of the workforce. To say the "87 per cent of us who are working" are better off implies a comparison with the same 87 per cent in 1979. But the middle-ranked (median) employee in 1979 was 9.5 million places away from the top of the ranking; whereas in 1986 he or she was only 8 million away. The person 9.5 million places away from the top would now be earning less than the person of the same rank in 1979, somewhere between the top-paid 50 per cent and the lowest-paid 25 per cent.

Lord Young's analysis glides over the fact that there were fewer jobs available which paid, the equivalent of say, £7,500 in 1986.

The separate figures for men and women tell very different stories. Most of those who are "worse off" on this basis are men — while the best-paid 1.4 million men (the top 10 per cent in 1979, top 12.3 per cent in 1986) were at least £2,500 a year better off in real terms. The figures for full-time women employees, whose number fell by only 300,000 or 6 per cent, show that the pay of nearly all those women still in work kept ahead of inflation, compared with the same-ranked women in 1979. [4]

After tax

What matters, however, is not simply "pay", but what's left in the pocket (after tax, National Insurance and child benefit) compared with inflation. Applying the same technique to figures obtained from Chancellor Nigel Lawson by Labour Shadow Leader of the House Peter Shore, the picture looks even worse, which isn't surprising, as the tax burden has increased under the Conservatives. There isn't any information about the earnings of part-timers and the self-employed. Furthermore, we don't know how male and female earners combine in two-earner and single-earner *households*, which is why a definitive answer is not possible to the question, how many of "us who are working" haven't never had it so good?

The partial evidence suggests that fewer than 70 per cent of all full-time employees in 1986 were better off in real terms (after tax, National Insurance and child benefit) than the best-off same number of employees in 1979. [5]

Buying off the marginal classes

Lord Young's complacency made public the Conservatives' compassionate electoral strategy: to buy off an electoral majority and get the rest off the register. There are about forty-five million votes around. Is it true that Mrs Thatcher has delivered greater prosperity to an electoral majority and damned the rest? The above figure-juggling suggests that the workforce and its dependants are divided much more evenly between the "better-off" and "worse-off" sides of the scales than Lord Young would have us think. The rest of the population balances something like this:

● Ten million pensioners — rich pensioners have done all right under Mrs Thatcher, as tax thresholds have gone up more than inflation, taxes on capital have been reduced, and the stock market has boomed. Not all of the five million old people getting a pension from their employer's fund have kept up with inflation, but each new "cohort" of people retiring is much better off than the dead pensioners they replace. On the debit side, the three million pensioners relying wholly or mainly on the state pension have only seen it updated by the Retail Prices Index, which doesn't reflect fully the price rises that affect them.

● Four million unemployed or on "schemes" — that's two and a half million more than in 1979.

● Half a million students — for the 1987/88 academic year, the grant was £1,972 a year, 21 per cent lower in real terms than in 1979.

Altogether the voters come out approximately 42 per cent better off, 45 per cent worse off and 13 per cent unchanged. Individuals aren't always able to see how broad categories are faring, as they may be glad to have a job at all, or they may have had their pay as an individual go up ahead of inflation year after year, with the occasional promotion. But it's not surprising that the government has a few problems getting the revivalist gospel across. Asked in June 1985 how "people like yourself" had done since the Conservatives came to power, 50 per cent said they were worse off, 22 per cent said better off and 26 per cent saw no difference. Even among ABC1s — the usually strongly Tory professional, managerial and clerical categories — 43 per cent said they were worse off and only 27 per cent better off (*The Gallup Survey of Britain*, p. 140).

The distribution of total income
The Department of Employment's New Earnings Survey provides information about the earned income of employees. However, to include the whole population in the assessment of income inequality, detailed information is needed about other income in the form of pensions, investment returns, state benefits and grants.

What is needed is a ranking for the distribution of all income among the whole population. What would be even better would be a ranking of after-tax income, as it is the final outcome that matters. The good news is that the Central Statistical Office does produce such figures. The bad news — apart from what they contain — is that they are produced on the basis of tax units, that is, men and their dependants. (Single women are treated as honorary and temporary men.) This means two-earner couples, one-earner couples and single people are all treated as one "unit". They also ignore National Insurance contributions, which are a backdoor income tax, falling proportionately more heavily on poorer earners. And, lastly, the government has saved money and shame by publishing them only once every three years, so the latest figures are only for 1981/82.

Forget those figures, for the moment, then. A more meaningful set of data has been produced by the Institute of Fiscal Studies from official figures (see Table 2). They illustrate the stark transfer of resources from the poorer half of the population to the richest tenth. The figures in Table 2 show the distribution of all after-tax income, adjusted to take account of each person's family circumstances: adult couples are assumed to need 1.6 times as much as a single adult to live at the equivalent standard, and children are assumed to need between a tenth and a fifth of a single adult's income, depending on age.[6] So although the figures don't show how much disposable income the average person in the top 10 per cent has (the actual amount would

---

TABLE 2
Distribution of All Income 1977–83

Percentage share of	1977	1983	Change (as percentage of 1977 share)
Top 10%	21.2	23.7	+11%
2nd 10%	14.8	15.0	+1%
3rd 10%	12.5	12.3	−2%
4th 10%	10.9	10.7	−2%
5th 10%	9.6	9.4	−3%
6th 10%	8.5	8.2	−4%
7th 10%	7.5	7.0	−7%
8th 10%	6.5	5.9	−9%
9th 10%	5.2	4.8	−8%
Bottom 10%	3.2	3.1	−3%

Earned and unearned income after tax and National Insurance, plus benefits; distribution among "equivalent" persons including children (see text); Great Britain.

Source: Nick Morris and Ian Preston, "Taxes, Benefits and the Distribution of Income 1968–83", *Fiscal Studies*, November 1986.

---

depend on how old they were and who they lived with), they do measure the real differences in spending power: the average person in the top 10 per cent was 7.5 times better off than the average in the bottom 10 per cent in 1983 (the gap had widened to 6.5 times in 1977).

These figures cover a six-year period including the last two years of the Callaghan government. The Central Statistical Office figures referred to above, although they aren't suitable for assessing the size of the gap between rich and poor, do confirm that all this reverse Robin Hoodism occurred after 1979. What's more, the Central Statistical Office figures reveal that the enrichment of the top 10 per cent was heavily skewed in favour of the top 1 per cent. In the first three years of the Thatcher government, despite the recession, the top 10 per cent of tax units (not the same as the top 10 per cent in Table 2) were 12 per cent better off after accounting for inflation; but the top 1 per cent were 22 per cent better off, the next 4 per cent 12 per cent richer and the next 5 per cent 8 per cent richer.[7]

What is going on? What's happening at the top is obvious, and we shall look at the top pay explosion in a moment. To try to understand what is happening in the rest of the population we have to turn to research by Michael O'Higgins at the University of Bath. The figures in Table 2 are derived from the Family Expenditure Survey, but it also provides all sorts of other detailed information about household types and family structures.

O'Higgins has analysed the changing make-up of the population at different levels of income from the FES computer tapes. His main finding is that retired people are getting richer and are moving up the income scale, while their place at the bottom of the pile is being taken by the unemployed. It's not of course that individual old people are getting greatly richer, but that each new generation of people retiring is better-off than the dying generation they replace, with many more of them having good pensions from their job. In 1979 three-quarters of the adults in the poorest 20 per cent of households were retired, but by 1984 only half were, and almost all of the other half were unemployed or "unoccupied".

What's really distressing about O'Higgins's research is that it shows that the number of children in the poorest 20 per cent of households has doubled: in 1979, 6 per cent of children were in the "bottom quintile"; in 1984, 13 per cent were.

There are, of course, a number of non-monetary benefits which should be weighed in the balance when assessing the distribution of income — the main ones being services such as education, health, and various subsidies, such as for housing and public transport.

The Central Statistical Office tries to measure these benefits and allocate them to households, to estimate inequality while taking into account all transactions between households and the public sector. The result is a series called "The Effect of Tax and Benefits on Household Income" published each December in *Economic Trends*. It's a crude way of measuring absolute rather than relative inequality: for example, in that everyone in Britain is entitled to health care, they are better off than many in the Third World. But this method isn't necessarily a good way of measuring inequality within a country.

The Central Statistical Office takes the distribution of "original income" — that is, income from "the market": wages, private sector pensions, income from wealth — then adds state benefits, then subtracts tax (including indirect taxes like VAT), and then adds state benefits in kind, to arrive at a distribution of "final income".

Apart from income tax and National Insurance contributions, this process has surprisingly little effect on the inequality of income. In 1984 the top fifth of households had 40 per cent of disposable income (after income tax, National Insurance and benefits) and 39 per cent of "final income". The share of the bottom fifth only rose from 6.7 per cent to 7.1 per cent.[8] Although the bottom households get most benefit in kind from state education, housing subsidy and welfare foods, households at the top do slightly better out of NHS spending and transport subsidies. They also pay less as a proportion of their disposable income in indirect taxes (the bottom fifth of households pay 29 per cent in indirect taxes, the top fifth pay 23 per cent — partly because they save more).

But the Central Statistical Office's approach implies that if A has NHS treatment costing the taxpayer £200 and B has private treatment costing her £300, A would be two-thirds as "rich" as B. But in reality A may have no money while B has £300, which she chooses to spend on health care. Treating amounts spent by the taxpayer on a person's health as their income (a benefit in kind, the Central Statistical Office calls it), doesn't work under a system of universal service provided on need. (In effect the prices paid for private health care and education are a premium people are prepared to pay for private instead of state provision, not instead of no provision at all.) The person who needs a £10,000 heart operation and gets it on the NHS is not £10,000 better off than a healthy person. More to the point, old people are not better off than young adults because they use more health care resources; they are worse off because they are more ill. (But they *are* better off in absolute terms than most old or young people in the Third World, for whom there are few health care resources at all.)[9]

Any analysis of how unequal a society is comes back to the democratic aspirations of its people, which is why there is a need for a relative definition of poverty and wealth, discussed further on p. 95. As Tories often point out, everybody is unequal. But some inequalities matter more than others, and some are fairer than others. A barely adequate health service or education service, provided to everybody as of right free of charge, is not enough to satisfy the moderate egalitarianism of the British electorate while growing numbers of people can afford to buy a better private service. Giving a "premium" service to more people while the "standard" service obtained by what remains the vast majority stays the same — let alone deteriorates — is actually slightly equalising in the Gini coefficient sense. But in that it increases the distance of that majority from the average, it affects the majority's sense of relative discrimination. When the occupants of the average (non-retired) household see someone paying £100 for a private varicose vein operation, they don't console themselves with the thought that the NHS spends £620 a year (in 1984) on them — after all, that's six times as much — they see someone jumping the queue with money they haven't got.

The Top Pay Explosion

> "You are not doing anything against the poor by
> seeing the top people are paid well."
> — Mrs Thatcher, July 1985.

One of the most remarkable developments since 1979 is that increase in the top 1 per cent's share of income. Between the Second World War and 1979, the top 1 per cent's share of income had halved. Part of this reduction was due to the reduction in the concentration of wealth, since about a fifth of the income of the top 1 per cent comes from wealth: interest, rent and dividends. The reversal in the trend in incomes is all the more remarkable for not being accompanied by an increase in the top 1 per cent's share of wealth.[10] The salaried rich have enjoyed an unprecedented Top Pay Explosion, with a more unequal share-out of earned income than at any time since before the Second World War. Official statistics only go up to 1983/84 (the

Inland Revenue's Survey of Personal Incomes), but a number of organisations conduct surveys of top management pay, and they all show that there's been no let-up in the "The-more-you've-got-the-more-you-get" factor.

All the surveys reported in the *Top Pay Review* published by Incomes Data Services show a similar pattern. As average earnings were rising steadily at an underlying rate of 7.5 per cent from 1983, managers' earnings have been rising — on average — by between 9 and 11 per cent a year. One of the biggest surveys, carried out by the British Institute of Management, showed that executive pay rose by 10.6 per cent in 1985 and 9.1 per cent in 1986. This may be only a few percentage points above the national average, but the annual extra increment of 1.5 to 3 per cent on salaries that are larger money amounts — the top tenth of men in 1986 were already those above £16,800 — has a cumulative effect.

What's more, the "to them that hath" principle applies all the way up, as differentials steadily widen. Charterhouse's six-monthly survey, *Top Management Remuneration*, showed that the average executive salaries were increasing at 10.5 per cent a year in August 1985 and 10.2 per cent a year in August 1986. But the range of increases widened over the two years, with a quarter of the sample getting rises of 17 per cent or more. And total earnings at the very top — chairpersons and chief executives — rose by even more (average up 11.6 per cent) and ranged even wider, a quarter getting rises of 23 per cent or more and one in ten getting at least 42 per cent. (This spreading out at the top is associated with the rapid spread of performance-related bonuses, and rises in basic salary have been consistently lower than for total earnings.)

In 1984, when I started to record top public company salaries, £100,000 a year was a very large, round number, which seemed the natural cut-off point for a "league table". In 1985 people earning £100,000 grew too numerous to list, and £150,000 became the qualification for business megastars. Now the league table uses £250,000 as its cut-off point in order to keep it to one page (and in Table 7 on p. 137 I've used £300,000 as the cut-off point). These are people earning more than the biggest premium bond prize every year. There were 688 directors and employees in the published company accounts on Charterhouse's database earning more than £100,000 in 1985/86 — a fifth of those estimated by the Inland Revenue to be earning that much: these are just the people whose salaries we know about because they're published in their company accounts.

Tony Vernon-Harcourt, the author of *Top Management Remuneration UK*, sums up in the 1985/86 edition the non-cash advantages of life at the top thus:

> The director and senior manager continue to receive a range of protective benefits — medical insurance, long-term ill health plan, pension, life assurance and a service contract. A car and private petrol will be provided.

All these perks have continued to spread among executives to the point that they are now considered "standard", and are now spreading in many cases to middle management and ordinary workers. But Vernon-Harcourt reports that "there are no signs that 'beyond the fringe' benefits — villas abroad, suit leasing schemes [sic] — are increasing in acceptability", although a revival had been predicted after the imposition of 10.45 per cent employer's National Insurance contributions on salaries over £13,780 in October 1985. He speculates that "administration costs may outweigh any savings". I think other explanations are more likely. One is that employers hadn't yet had time to respond to the change. Another is that some of the wilder tales of tax avoidance mythology were in response to high marginal rates of *income tax*. National Insurance contributions are easier to get round, because unlike income tax they aren't levied on benefits in kind, such as holidays, insurance and company cars. But another reason could be that the more exotic perks are no longer needed. Not because executives are satisfied with their bloated pay packets, but because they've now got the perk of all perquisites. Who needs to worry about Luncheon Vouchers (tax free up to 75p a week)? They've got share options: direct injections of capital gained on multiples of their earnings and taxed at half rate (see p. 66).

Share option schemes can produce a profit equivalent to more than a year's salary if a company's shares merely keep up with inflation. A director on a salary of £45,000, granted options over £100,000-worth of shares, can make a profit equivalent to a cash payment of £48,350 after five years, if the share price only keeps up with inflation at 5 per cent.[11] Executive share options are a payout to the already well paid, partly at the expense of the taxpayer, partly at the expense of shareholders, who, although they may *want* to pay directors more to achieve results, don't know how much they are paying. The cost isn't shown in the accounts because it isn't borne by the company but directly by other shareholders. (Share options involve the issue of new shares, which slightly reduce the value of all shares already on the market.)

According to Vernon-Harcourt, the lack of information share-holders — let alone the general public — can obtain about cash bonus systems is even worse. "Very few companies disclose any useful information and there's nothing shareholders can do about it apart from getting up at the annual general meeting and asking a question which needn't be answered." This is shareholder democracy. The whole system relies on shareholders not asking questions when companies are doing well, and informal nods, mutterings and raised eyebrows in the right quarters when they're not.

The bloating of "executive remuneration" is also distorting the labour market. Headhunters say that burgeoning option schemes have begun to make it difficult for "top" people to move. The build-up of tax-subsidised piles of potential capital off the profit-and-loss account means that recruiting companies can't match rewards. Options in the poaching company can't be offered at below the market price without the difference being charged to profits (just like salary). So the longer executives stay with their company, the harder it is for poachers to match their gains.

Golden Handshakes
Golden handshakes are not exactly income, but part of the "remuneration package". Most golden boy is Sir Michael Edwardes, who picked up an estimated £200,000 when Dunlop was taken over by Sir Owen Green's conglomerate, BTR, in 1985 (although his contract said he was entitled to £390,000). He tops the charts by adding this to his £383,000 payoff from British computer-makers ICL in 1983. He's now chair and chief executive of Chloride battery makers.

Golden handshakes hit the headlines in the early 1980s as the recession struck and companies retrenched. Then they faded from view, with the occasional record figures being noted. Suddenly, they are back in fashion. The current record is held by Anthony Edgar, who left Ratners jewellers after four months as chairperson with a cheque for £550,000, after his family sold H. Samuel to Ratners in 1986 and Edgar fell out with Gerald Ratner who took over the business from his father in 1984. Gerald, who took over as chair-person as well as chief executive, said: "It's a hell of a sum — like winning the pools — but it is what his and our lawyers agreed was the right figure."

Peter Laister was paid off as chair and chief executive of Thorn EMI in July 1985 with £440,000. But the most extravagant package of recent times (because of all the extras thrown in) was the £407,386 payoff to Sir Ronald Halstead, dismissed as chair and chief executive of drugs company Beecham in November 1985. In a most un-British display of brute corporate muscle he was ousted by Lord Keith of Castleacre after fifteen weeks as chairperson for failing to do anything about Beecham's inadequate profits. He was on a salary of around £200,000 when he got the chop, so that's only two years' pay (or 129 years' Supplementary Benefit at the long-term rate for married couples). But the rules of the company's share option scheme also allowed him to exercise his options, producing a useful nest-egg for his "early retirement" of up to £70,000. But you can't just turn a man onto the streets with half a million in his pocket. So Beecham also agreed to pay him an early pension of £90,000 a year. Then to add insult to injury the company appointed the American vice-chair of Textron in his place for $1 million a year — £690,000 — briefly making him the highest-paid British-resident director.

What's behind this sudden bonanza for sacked executives? It's one of those "standard" perks, service contracts. Rare until the 1980s, service contracts are one of those extremely useful low visibility perks, like share options, that no one really notices until the fruit machine pours forth for the lucky winner. At first glance to the innocent shareholder there doesn't seem to be anything inherently wicked about senior executives having their terms and conditions of employment in writing. But service contracts are more than just contracts of employment: they specify a term of service, such as three or five years. If for any reason short of criminal insanity the executive leaves the company — for example, after a boardroom row — before this term is up, the company has to pay several years' "notice". Anthony Edgar's service contract had four years to run, and he was on a salary of £140,000, hence his chart-topping payoff.

Recent golden handshakes have illustrated how unjustifiable service contracts are. A salary of over £100,000 is insupportable on any moral grounds, but a lump sum multiple of it for performing badly doesn't even make capitalist sense.

The Growth of Poverty

"People on modest incomes" — DHSS minister
John Major describing those on or just above
Supplementary Benefit levels, July 1986.

The last section looked at how well top earners have done in the past few years. Their success has been matched by an increase in poverty — not so much in the sense that the poor have become poorer, but in that there are now many millions more of them.

Two days after the Royal Wedding, which doubled Prince Andrew's Civil List income to £50,000 a year, a lookout posted by Labour MP Frank Field spotted the arrival of some papers in the House of Commons library. The library was just about to close for the three-month summer recess, but there was time to take a photocopy and within hours Field was on to the media with a coup that foiled the government's plan to conceal the publication of figures showing the rise in poverty during the first Thatcher administration.

The figures were the official DHSS estimates of the numbers of people in Great Britain living at, below and just above the Supplementary Benefit level for 1983. As with the overall income distribution figures, the government had reduced the frequency of publication, in this case to every other year. The 1981 figures had shown a sharp increase over 1979, but the 1983 figures were more than eighteen months late. The government had had them for some time, but was unable to doctor them in any way and was desperate to soften the impact of publishing.

Whether the clash with The Wedding was intentional or not, the government's business managers used it to rush a lot of image-rotting legislation through the House of Commons, most notably reversing the Lords' attempts to keep the "well" in "welfare state". (The Lords had chucked out a clause to make claimants pay a fifth of their rates bill, no matter how poor, and inserted one to make Social Fund payments grants not loans.)

But the plan to avoid publicity over the "poverty" figures relied on more than distracting the populace with the latest episode of *Palace*. Frank Field had already asked for the figures (lots of times), and was expecting the government to try to sneak them out at the end of the session, and so had put down a question for answer on the last day to make sure the government couldn't avoid telling him when the figures were put in the library (a way of "publishing" documents without making them widely available). The government's counter ploy was nearly successful. Tory MP Edwina Currie had asked a planted question which junior DHSS minister John Major answered, saying the figures had been placed in the library. His answer to Frank Field's question simply referred him to his reply to Edwina Currie — an answer that wasn't published until after the library was closed. Using the "plant" was an attempt to postpone alerting Field until after the library closed for the summer, while still technically publishing the figures.

The government also intended to take advantage of the royal nuptials to publish the 1982/83 figures for death rates of different social classes. Although the figures had been ready since the beginning of 1986, they were eventually scheduled for publication on Wedding Day. At the last minute publication was delayed for six days, until after the Commons had recessed. Labour MPs had already made a fuss about the plan to force through anti-poor legislation on the day of the Wedding — a fuss that was reported in the media — so it might have been judged counter-productive to publish damning health inequality figures on the same date. When they *were* published, the crucial numbers were left out of the main report, and had to be calculated by journalists from the crude data on microfiches, which were priced at £46 and which need special equipment to read.

But what did those "poverty" figures show? In 1983 there were 8.9 million people in Great Britain on or below the Supplementary Benefit level, which is now £29.80 a week (£1,550 a year) for a single person and £48.40 (£2,517 a year) for a couple, excluding housing costs, child additions and one-off special needs payments. The long-term rate for people on Supplementary Benefit for over a year, or for those over sixty, is £37.90 a week (£1,971 a year) or £60.65 a week (£3,154 a year) for couples. The numbers of people with this level of income or less rose from 6.1 million in 1979, and an estimate by the statistical section of the House of Commons library suggests that the figure had risen to at least 11.9 million in the UK in 1986. That is one in every five people.

The DHSS figures also showed that there were another 7.5 million people in Great Britain with incomes up to 40 per cent greater than the Supplementary Benefit level in 1983. The significance of this level is that it includes people on Unemployment Benefit (which is a few pence a week higher than Supplementary Benefit), and the 3.8 million on state pensions who have no other significant income (the state pension is only 40p a week more than long-term Supplementary Benefit for a single person or 65p more for a couple). It also catches 4 million people in families of the working poor, most of whom live on incomes above the basic Supplementary Benefit rate, but many of whom subsist on incomes below or not much higher than the long-term Supplementary Benefit rate, which is 26 per cent above the basic Supplementary Benefit rate. [12]

The government does not, of course, accept that these figures indicate the level of poverty. (It is quite right; the findings of the *Breadline Britain* survey show that they *underestimate* poverty as most people would understand it: see p. 97.) Instead they are officially known as the numbers of those on "low incomes". In the furore over the publication of the 1983 figures, John Major, junior DHSS minister, in a further development of Tory Newspeak, talked of "people who live on modest incomes". Updated to 1986, the number of people either on Supplementary Benefit or on other modest incomes was a grotesque total of around twenty million.

In dismal justification John Major clutched at an interesting straw. The Supplementary Benefit level, he said, had gone up by "around 6 per cent" more than inflation, and so it was bound to catch more people. This would, he said, account for about one-third of the increase in the figures. So on the government's own admission (the basis for John Major's claim isn't known), fully two-thirds of the increase in the numbers of those on low incomes is an increase in real terms.

But drawing attention to the effect of inflation only bounces back in John Major's face — inflation has hit the poor harder than the rich under this as under previous governments. The only elaboration on John Major's statement that the DHSS press office was able to offer was that the calculation was arrived at after excluding housing costs from the Retail Prices Index (RPI), as claimants have their rent paid by the DHSS. And housing costs have been one of the causes of "differential inflation" since 1979, as council rents have gone up by more than average inflation. But the Institute for Fiscal Studies' analysis of the RPI shows that it is mostly the faster-than-average rises in the prices of basics such as food, clothes and heat that have imposed a 5 per cent inflationary surcharge on the poorest households compared with the richest between 1974 and 1982. [13]

Although Supplementary Benefit rates for children have risen well ahead of inflation, adult rates (measured against the RPI, excluding housing costs) rose by less than 2 per cent in "real terms" between

1979 and 1986. The short-term rates have risen by just under 2 per cent, while the long-term rates for single people and couples have risen by 1 and 2 per cent respectively. This is easily wiped out — and reversed — by the higher inflation rate for the poor. The government should be given credit for substantially increasing the value of child rates of Supplementary Benefit. But even if claimants generally — and there are many more of them with children — have seen a very small improvement in Supplementary Benefit, the *Breadline Britain* survey (p. 99) suggests that between 13 and 21 per cent of the adult population is excluded from what is by common consent full participation in society.

---

1. Central Statistical Office *Economic Trends*, second quarter 1979 to second quarter 1986, divided by total population. Real personal disposable income per person aged 15 or over rose by only 8 per cent. Between 1981/82 and the second quarter 1986, this figure rose by 7 per cent.

2. The figures for all employees (men and women together) for 1979 are not published, because those for men and women were not then strictly compatible (men are over eighteens, women over twenty-ones) so I have estimated combined figures for 1979 on the basis of the separate figures for men and women, the relationship between those for men and women separately and together in 1985, and adjusting for the fact that there were proportionately more men in the workforce in 1979.

3. If we put employees in rank order and take the earnings of the woman (or, less probably, man) one tenth of the way up from the bottom, this is called the bottom "decile". Now quantiles, as they are known — you can have deciles which divide the population up into tenths, quartiles which divide it into quarters, or quintiles which divide it up into fifths, like the median which cuts off the top and bottom halves — are useful tools of analysis, but easily misunderstood and indeed easily used to mislead. The bottom decile is not the same as the bottom tenth, which is properly called the "bottom decile group"; it is the level below which the bottom tenth of all earners or wealth holders fall. The Great Decile Con Trick, where you compare the bottom (or top) decile of a different number of earners, has caught out even competent commentators like the Economics Correspondent of the *Guardian*, who once wrote an article called "The Rich Push the Poor Out of Work" (11 April 1985). He didn't know the half of it. Worse, he confused "decile" with "tenth", saying that the pay of the bottom 10 per cent of male earners fell by 0.2 per cent in real terms 1979 – 84, when he meant that the bottom decile point fell by 0.2 per cent (that is, the pay of those in the bottom 10 per cent probably fell by *at least* 0.2 per cent).

4. These calculations are based on straight-line interpolations of New Earnings Survey data, April 1979 and April 1986, against the Retail Prices Index for the relevant months. They are therefore approximate, but the shape of the distributions means that in the middle a straight line is as good as any other curve. Both New Earnings Survey data and Labour Force Surveys, from which the changes in the size of the workforce are taken, are for Great Britain only.

5. Using straight-line interpolation (as Note 4) of figures given in a Parliamentary Answer (*Hansard*, 1 December 1986), between 30 and 35 per cent of the 1986 numbers of full-time male employees were worse off after deductions and child benefit; or 50 per cent of the 1979 numbers. The pattern is almost identical for a single man, a married man with children, or without children (with a wife not earning). Figures for single women show that all are better off on this basis.

6. The main problem with the Central Statistical Office figures is that they apply to tax units rather than individuals and therefore don't give a proper indication of the gap between the top and bottom of British society. For instance, an average tax unit in the top 10 per cent in 1981/82 had an income of £12,763 (after tax) whereas the average in the bottom 10 per cent was £1,190. This doesn't mean people at the top got ten times as much as people at the bottom. The top tax unit could have been a woman with a salary of £10,000 (before tax) and her husband on £6,500 a year, while the bottom tax unit was quite likely to be a single teenager on the dole.

Hence the use of "equivalence scales" to adjust for people's different family circumstances. The IFS analysis in Table 2 uses the values implied by the Supplementary Benefit rates (a couple gets £48.40, which is 1.6 times a single person's benefit of £29.80 a week). The Royal Commission on the Distribution of Income and Wealth examined the question of equivalence scales and tested values of between 1.33 and 2 for adult couples (taking single adults as 1), and between .11 and .16 for children, which in different combinations raised the lower quartile as a proportion of the median by between 21 and 28 per cent, compared with the income distribution before it was adjusted (*Report No 6*, "Lower Incomes", Cmnd. 7175, HMSO 1978, p. 172). This suggests that adjustments using equivalence scales make a difference, but that the exact values used are not very important.

7. The Central Statistical Office series of statistics on which the Table 2a below is based combines the data from the Survey of Personal Incomes and the Family Expenditure Survey (thus remedying one of the defects of the figures in Table 2, which is that they are based on a small sample of 7,000 households, after a 30 per cent non-response level which exacerbates the problem of under-reported income in high-income households). This table is published in *Economic Trends* under the heading "The distribution of income in the UK". The figures cover each year from 1949 to 1978/79 (changing from calendar years to financial years in 1976), and is now three-

TABLE 2a

Distribution of All Income Among Tax Units

	Share of net income 1981/82 (%)	Real change since 1978/79 (%)
Top 1%	4.4	+22
Next 4%	10.4	+12
Next 5%	9.9	+8
Top 10%	24.7	+12
2nd 10%	15.7	+4
3rd 10%	12.8	0
4th 10%	10.7	−2
5th 10%	8.9	−3
6th 10%	7.6	−1
7th 10%	6.6	+3
8th 10%	5.4	+2
9th 10%	4.4	+3
Bottom 10%	2.9	−16

Earned and unearned income after tax (but before deducting National Insurance), plus benefits, UK.

Source: Central Statistical Office, author's calculations to adjust for effects of changing numbers of adults and of excluding part-year incomes.

yearly. The figures for 1981/82 were published in July 1984. Those for 1983/84 are expected in July 1987. Using unpublished data supplied by the Central Statistical Office, I've calculated the change in the after-tax income of various percentages of the population after taking inflation, and changes in the composition of tax units, into account. The second column in Table 2a shows the change in the real amount of after-tax income going to the same groups over the three years. The size of the whole cake rose by only 2.5 per cent because of the 1980 recession, but the table shows what variations this sort of bland statistic can conceal. Since 1981/82 personal disposable income per adult has risen by about 7 per cent in real terms by mid-1986 (see Note 1); this is no guarantee that the poorest are better off.

The figures in the first column have been adjusted in line with the effect of excluding part-year incomes on the 1978/79 figures (the detailed calculations were not provided for 1981/82 by the Central Statistical Office). The figures in the second column show the percentage change in the real income of each group (against the Retail Prices Index) after making an allowance for the 2 per cent increase in the total number of adults. The Central Statistical Office was unable to provide information on the change in the composition of tax units at different levels, but did supply overall totals of single people (15,443 in 1978/79 and 16,563 in 1981/82) and couples (13,633 and 13,455).

8. Re-ranking households at each stage. "The Effects of Taxes and Benefits on Household Income 1984", *Economic Trends*, July 1986.

9. State education is different, because it's not allocated on the basis of need, but, after the age of sixteen, on "merit". Comprehensive education was an attempt to eliminate the division in the state sector on the basis of this dubious concept of merit below the age of sixteen, but several such divisions still exist above that age: A-levels versus leaving school, universities versus polytechnics, Oxbridge versus other universities. Different kinds of education cost different amounts to provide, but each division is also directly related to later financial inequalities.

10. Given the real rise in house prices, which benefits those outside the richest 1 per cent in greater proportion, the distribution of other, income-producing assets has probably become more concentrated, as the overall proportional distribution has stayed the same; and yields from capital have increased. But most of the top 1 per cent's increase in income share has been in income from employment.

11. £100,000 is a fairly typical figure and the maximum eligible for tax relief. If the shares only keep pace with inflation at 5 per cent a year, they'd be worth £127,629 after five years. This £27,629 profit is equivalent to a cash payment of £48,350 because of the tax relief, being taxed at the 30 per cent Capital Gains Tax rate instead of the 60 per cent top income tax rate, which someone on £45,000 a year might be paying if their accountant can't find enough tax dodges.

12. The figures are by no means straightforward. They are derived from the Family Expenditure Survey, and estimate the numbers of people and families in three groups: those in receipt of Supplementary or Housing Benefit; those *not* in receipt of these benefits whose income after tax, National Insurance, housing costs and fares to work (if employed) is less than short-term Supplementary Benefit, or long-term Supplementary Benefit if they are over pension age; and those whose income on this basis is less than 140 per cent of the relevant Supplementary Benefit level. Hence there is no single "Supplementary Benefit level". The maximum disposable income of a single person covered by "the poverty figures" (excluding child additions and special needs payments) is £2,759 a year (40 per cent more than the long-term Supplementary Benefit rate), or £4,415 for a couple.

13. Vanessa Fry and Panos Pashardes, *The RPI and the Cost of Living*, Institute for Fiscal Studies 1986. The index of average prices paid by households at the lowest decile of "original" income (market income, excluding state benefits) was 323.4 in January 1982 (January 1974 = 100), whereas that at the highest decile was 306.5, or 5.5 per cent less.

4. INEQUALITY OF WEALTH

"Despite the welfare state the key pillars of social
and economic inequality remain intact. While the
very rich have lost some of their riches to the less
rich, over time, the poor have hardly profited
proportionately."— Neil Kinnock, *The Future of
Socialism*, Fabian Society lecture,
November 1985. [1]

The previous chapter describes what has happened to income distribution since 1979. The conclusion is that income distribution has
become considerably more unequal, as the top 10 (and especially top
1) per cent have increased their share while the numbers on
Supplementary Benefit have grown.

But there has been no equivalent trend in the distribution of
wealth. The share of the rich has remained static, which — although
it represents a change from the gently declining share of the
wealthiest 1 per cent during this century — might seem surprising. In
fact the figures for shares of total wealth contain an optical illusion.
Since total personal wealth has increased, and the share of the rich
has remained the same, they have seen large increases in their
holdings — many times larger than the increases enjoyed by those at
the average level of increased wealth.

Disbelief is the usual response on the Left when faced with official
estimates of wealth distribution which show no increase in
proportional inequality between 1979 and 1984. How can it be,
people ask, that in the first five years of Thatcherism, with tax breaks
and soaring incomes for the rich, they didn't increase their share of
wealth? "Yes, well, those figures are unreliable," is one possible
answer. "I simply don't believe them," says one commentator. It's a
response reinforced by the at first sight bizarre way the Inland
Revenue estimates are calculated. Everyone who dies in a particular
year is treated as a sample of the living, and their wealth, as reported
for the purposes of Inheritance Tax, forms the basis of an elaborate
display of computer skills.

Dead people are not a very representative sample, it's true. A lot of
them were old, and likely to be richer than average, and very few
were both young and rich, although the sample for 1986 will include

the estate of Olivia Channon, scion of the Guinness dynasty, valued at £500,000 when she died aged twenty-two. But the sample is divided into age, sex and class groups, and multiplied up so that it represents the whole (living) population. The latest estimates use a new computer program which creates a whole imaginary adult population using death tax statistics as clues. Obviously the wealth of older people is more accurately estimated, but there are enough younger people dying each year to produce a coherent picture.

Most people don't pay any tax when they die, and a report only has to be made to the Inland Revenue if you have assets worth more than £5,000. So the wealth of the poorer half of the population has to be estimated from other figures such as for savings and consumer goods. Conservatives used to criticise the Inland Revenue's figures because they didn't include estimates for the poorer half, and so made Britain seem more unequal than it was. When the Revenue started to estimate for the whole adult population, it didn't make much difference. In 1984, for instance, the average adult in the poorer half owned marketable assets worth just £2,140. (The average in the richer half was £33,580.)

Another form of wealth that doesn't appear in death tax returns has to be added in. The Inland Revenue estimates that in 1982 assets worth £22,000 million were held in discretionary trusts — almost all on behalf of the richest 1 per cent. Trusts which disburse money at the "discretion" of their trustees are a popular way of benefiting from wealth without legally owning it. (Although this is a vast sum of money, it could well be an underestimate: it's an increase of only 5 per cent over the 1981 estimate and the Revenue admits that until fuller tax information from the "periodic charge" on discretionary trusts that is just beginning to come in can be analysed, it won't know how good an estimate it is.) And one form of wealth has to be subtracted: insurance policies that pay out on death, which can't be described as the wealth of the dead person when she or he was alive (although some insurance policies are part of savings plans, which are counted).

This is in fact the only way in which accurate estimates of the distribution of wealth can be made. Several European countries only have estimates derived from surveys, which are so unreliable as to be useless. People interviewed about their wealth either don't know, forget things or won't say how rich they are. Even well-designed surveys which over-sample the rich (to compensate for the fact that there are very few of them) have been shown to under-record a wide range of assets. A detailed dissection of a 1970 Canadian wealth survey (where sample information could be matched to tax records) found that the value of share holdings had been underestimated by 80 per cent, and the average underestimation for all assets was 34 per cent.[2]

In Britain, the Inland Revenue's death-duty-based estimate was only £13,000 million short of the Central Statistical Office's estimate of total personal wealth in 1982 (£796,000 million). One and a half per cent isn't a bad margin of error when dealing with such huge sums derived from different sources (and the errors are just as likely to be in the Central Statistical Office's figures as the Revenue's). The resulting estimates of the distribution of wealth are probably the most accurate in the world. They owe a lot to the work of two of the most rigorous and sceptical social scientists, Tony Atkinson and Alan Harrison, in the 1970s, and in particular to their critique of the old Inland Revenue estimates in the definitive book on the subject, *The Distribution of Personal Wealth in Britain* published in 1978. Their research was taken up by the Royal Commission on the Distribution of Income and Wealth, which may have been the 1974–79 Labour government's substitute for action on the subject, but ensured that at least the next Labour government will know exactly the scale of the task it faces.

The historical trend towards (but always a long way away from) equality during this century saw the share of personal wealth owned by the top 1 per cent of adults fall from about three-fifths in the 1920s to one-fifth by 1979; the proportion owned by the next 4 per cent stayed at about another one fifth, while the rest of the top half steadily increased its share from one-fifth to three-fifths. That trend was halted abruptly in 1979, and the shares of wealth remained unchanged until 1984, the last year for which figures are available. The distribution of wealth, excluding pension rights, during the first five years of Thatcherdom is summarised in Table 3 (p. 44).

London Weekend Television's *Fortune* programme (August 1986) commissioned Professor Tony Shorrocks to project the wealth distribution to 1986. He predicted no significant change in shares, and calculated that by 1986 there were 20,000 millionaires and multi-millionaires (0.05 per cent of all adults), who alone owned 4 per cent of total wealth.[3]

How unequal is this? International comparisons are one yardstick — Britain now has a similar level of wealth inequality to other industrialised countries for which there is reliable evidence.[4]

TABLE 3

Distribution of Wealth 1979 – 84

Percentage share of		Must have at least (1986)
Top 1%	21	£190,000
Top 2%	27	£120,000
Top 5%	39	£75,000
Top 10%	53	£50,000
Top 25%	76	£24,000
Top 50%	94	£8,000
Bottom 50%	6	average £2,500 each

Adult population, UK, personal wealth including house, excluding pension rights.

Source: *Inland Revenue Statistics 1984, 1986*, averages (Series C); projections to 1986 by Professor Anthony Shorrocks, Essex University (top 1, 5, 10 per cent), and calculated by the author.[5]

Another measure would be the distribution of wealth in a hypothetical egalitarian society — assuming that private property isn't abolished. Professor Tony Atkinson has calculated that if everyone earned the same, and saved at the same rate, and gifts and inheritance were banned, the richest 10 per cent of the population would have 19 per cent of total personal wealth, purely on the basis of having saved up for longer. Instead, the richest 10 per cent own 52 per cent of personal wealth. Estimates were commissioned by the Royal Commission, based on more realistic assumptions: existing unequal incomes, but assuming it were only possible to acquire wealth through saving. The share of the richest 1 per cent would then be between 3 and 7 per cent, depending on assumptions about interest rates — instead of 17 per cent of total personal wealth including private-sector pensions, which are a form of saving. Most of the difference is inheritance.[6]

The Inland Revenue produces three series of estimates, one (Table 3) excluding pension rights altogether, one including private-sector pension rights and one also including state pension rights. A private-sector pension is certainly a kind of wealth: it represents a claim over specific resources, against which the fund member can borrow and over which she or he might have some limited control. It provides a sense of security. And for some highly-paid executives, a "top hat" pension scheme is simply a tax shelter for substantial wealth. This is especially true in the case of self-employed people, who can have self-administered pension schemes (which can even be lent back into their businesses). In other senses, though, it isn't wealth. You can't sell it, and (apart from the lump sum) it can only be enjoyed in the form of income.

As two-fifths of adults are in occupational pension schemes (pensions that go with their job), including their pension rights in the calculation of the distribution of wealth makes the proportions more equal, reducing the share of the top 1 per cent to 17 per cent, but only increasing the share of the bottom half to 8 per cent.

Adding state pension rights — to which all National Insurance contributors are entitled — has an even more dramatic effect, cutting the share of the top 1 per cent to 12 per cent and increasing that of the bottom half to 17 per cent.[7] This is a much more dubious exercise, as there is little difference (40p a week or 65p for a couple) between a "right" to a state pension and a "right" to Supplementary Benefit for old people with no other major source of income. Since everyone is *in extremis* entitled to one or the other, an entitlement to a basic state pension hardly affects your relative position. However, the State Earnings-Related Pension Scheme (SERPS) provides an extra element to the basic pension which could be regarded as a separate store of wealth, but no estimates have been made treating *only* the extra earnings-related supplement as wealth, but not the basic state pension.

The only possible use for this third series of estimates is for presentational purposes, to soften the brutal contours of the wealth gradient in official statistics. There are arguments for and against including private-sector pensions in the assessment of wealth distribution, which ultimately depend on what you want to use the wealth distribution figures for; but in any case, the important point is that the trend in all three series is unmistakeably and stubbornly flat, showing no statistically significant change over the five years. The second part of the next chapter investigates the reasons why the distribution of wealth didn't become more unequal between 1979 and 1984.

---

1. Published as Fabian tract 509, January 1986.

2. J.B. Davies, "On the Size Distribution of Wealth in Canada", *Review of Income and Wealth*, 1979, cited by Alan Harrison, *The Distribution of Wealth*

in Ten Countries (see Bibliography on p. 185), p. 24.

3. The estimate for the number of millionaires rose from 13,000 in 1983, which indicates the effect of inflation and the steepness of the wealth gradient more than the Thatcher enrichment. The Inland Revenue revised its 1980−83 estimates of the distribution of wealth in September 1986, reducing its estimates of the numbers of rich people (those with more than £100,000) in 1983 by about 10 per cent, from about 760,000 to 680,000. Professor Shorrocks's projections were based on the unrevised 1983 figures. The detailed unrevised figures for 1983 were:

£200,000 − £300,000	116,000 people
£300,000 − £400,000	50,000
£400,000 − £500,000	24,000
£500,000 − £1,000,000	45,000
£1,000,000 − £2,000,000	8,000
£2,000,000 +	5,000

(Net wealth excluding pension rights, Series C. Source: special data provided by Inland Revenue.)

4. See Note 3, Chapter 2, on p. 20.

5. Author's estimates for thresholds of richest 2, 25 and 50 per cent derived by straight-line log normal interpolation of Inland Revenue (1986) estimates of 1984 distribution, revalued at 10 per cent a year, or of Professor Shorrocks's estimates.

6. A.B. Atkinson, "The Distribution of Wealth and the Individual Life-Cycle" (1971), in *Social Justice and Public Policy*, Wheatsheaf Books 1983; Royal Commission on the Distribution of Income and Wealth, *Reports No 5* and *7*, 1977 and 1979.

7. Because we don't know how private-sector pension rights are distributed (although we can work out how much they're worth in total), the Inland Revenue provides a range of estimates for the share of the bottom 90 per cent of adults. The "optimistic" assumption is that occupational pension rights are spread equally among pension scheme members of the same age. I have used the "pessimistic" assumption, which assumes they are spread in proportion to people's share of other (marketable) wealth.

5. "I BLAME THE GOVERNMENT"

The causes of income inequality

> "I do feel very strongly indeed that people on
> comparatively low wages and pensioners pay too
> much tax. You see 41 per cent of our income tax
> comes from those who earn average male
> earnings or less"
> — Mrs Thatcher, *Newsnight*, 30 July 1985.

The rich have got richer then. Their share of total income has increased since 1979, and while their proportional holdings of personal wealth have remained stable, this conceals large money increases. Why this reversal of the snail-like crawl towards greater equality?

It's becoming fashionable on the Left to emphasise the limits to the power of political parties and governments. But it is government policy, directly or indirectly, that has been responsible for much of the growth of inequality since 1979. The near tripling of unemployment is the single most important cause of greater inequality of income. But two things have also been happening to the incomes of those in work. First, the tax system has shifted some of the income of middle groups to the top few per cent and, secondly, underlying differentials have widened.

The first is government intervention in its most direct form, although the government says that it has only "allowed" the hard-working, the spirited and the ingenious to prosper, to keep what is theirs. "Let our children grow tall," as Mrs Thatcher so succinctly put it. This is permissiveness Tory style: if you can get rich and stay rich, be our guest. If you can't, don't let's inquire too closely into the reasons — after all, we don't want the state to interfere, do we?

However, for Chancellors Howe and Lawson to permit the rich to keep more of "their" money is no different *in outcome* from giving them some of "our" money. Tory philosophers argue that it's not just outcome that matters — that if the state steps in to take too large a slice of what people think they are *entitled* to, they will lack incentive, slow down and stop creating wealth and jobs. That's an argument which will be examined in Chapter 6, but for the purposes of explaining how Britain became a more unequal country, there's no difference between "causing" and "allowing" greater inequality.

Conservatives argue that the rich are "naturally" richer since 1979 because of *reduced* state intervention in the distribution of incomes. This is not so. The total tax burden has *increased* since 1979 — it has been shifted from the rich to the middling and poor — while the number of people dependent on the state for their income has also increased (despite the pushing of state employees into the private sector through privatisation and civil service cuts). The tax burden has been shifted from the rich and very rich to those on lower and middle incomes — and the total burden has become heavier as those on lower and middle incomes support rising numbers of those on incomes paid out of taxes.

For the grateful rich, who'd been playing dead in the hope that Chancellor Healey would go away and tax someone else, the new era was signalled by a massive one-off rise in their take-home pay as top tax rates were cut. In 1979, the top rate of income tax on earnings was cut from 83 per cent to 60 per cent. The effect on someone earning £50,000 (worth £86,000 in 1986) was to lift take-home pay from £17,000 to £27,000 — a remarkable 58 per cent rise, not to mention any annual pay rise on top.[1] How this happened can be seen by looking at the amount left after tax at the top rate: instead of taking home 17p in the pound of income above a certain amount, the highly paid were now taking home 40p per pound of high income.

That first tax cut was the most dramatic, but it was just the start of a series of tax changes which have benefited a tiny minority of the richest taxpayers. If the tax system had stayed the same as in 1978/79, taking inflation into account, then the richest few per cent of the population would have paid about £3,600 million more in taxes in 1986/87 than they did. That year's tax perk was worth about £15,000 to individuals on twenty times average earnings (£177,000 a year in 1986/87). Meanwhile, if social security policy had stayed the same as in May 1979 — most importantly retaining the pensions link with average earnings — the government would have paid £2,800 million more than it did in 1986/87, or about £180 per pensioner and benefit claimant.[2]

The Tax Subsidy System

Before 1979, if you believed that something called the "money supply" caused inflation, you were also likely to believe everything else that came out of the Chicago School of economics, personified in Austrian economist Friedrich Hayek, such as that tax reliefs were a form of public spending. (Not collecting an amount of tax has the same effect on the government's accounts as spending the same amount of public money: a point now widely accepted on the Left.) Not only were they a form of public spending, and hence a Bad Thing, but they were a crime against "fiscal neutrality", favouring some forms of economic activity over others, thus distorting free-market decisions, hence a Very Bad Thing Indeed.

Times change. First Mrs Thatcher was elected, and tax reliefs and allowances spread — as an interim measure to encourage free markets to work better. Then time went on, and money supply figures, after extensive genealogical research and several blood tests, turned out not to be even distantly related to the inflation figures. And nothing more was heard about tax reliefs being a kind of public spending.

Curiously, every single new tax relief, tax perk or tax subsidy introduced in Britain since 1979 has benefited the rich more than the poor. A hotch-potch of reliefs is now available to thrifty Supplementary Benefit claimants wanting to invest in new and small businesses under the Business Expansion Scheme (which offers income tax relief when you put your money in and Capital Gains Tax relief when you take it out again); or in large businesses whose shares are quoted on the Stock Exchange, through Personal Equity Plans (that offer income tax relief on dividends and Capital Gains Tax relief when you take your money out); or in a pension (income tax relief when you put your money in, income tax and Capital Gains Tax relief while it's in); or in a house (income tax relief on the rent you don't have to pay, Capital Gains Tax relief when you sell); or in government securities (Capital Gains Tax relief when sold); and so on.

It's not of course just the new reliefs that benefit the rich more than the poor. The reliefs that survived the last Labour government have the same effect. The fact that you don't pay income tax on contributions to a pension fund is exploited more by those who can afford to make large contributions. Inland Revenue figures show that the value of the relief rises as a proportion of income as income rises.[3] And even the *Financial Times* has admitted: "It is true that personal or corporate pension schemes allow possibly too generous tax shelter to be provided to earners of very high incomes."

Meanwhile, as we've seen, the underlying distribution of earned incomes *before tax* has also become sharply more unequal, as top pay explodes and the low paid strive, not always successfully, to keep up with inflation, let alone average earnings. Until this government came to power, it had become accepted in academic circles that wage differentials in the British or any other economy are extremely resistant to change. The consensus was that the shape and the spread of differentials in earned income was more or less fixed, and would return to its previous shape within a few years of receiving a "shock", such as a government incomes policy. Indeed, differentials didn't change through years of incomes policies in the 1970s.[4] Ironically it was a statistician called A.R. Thatcher who demonstrated in 1968 that the differentials for male manual workers in Britain had not changed since the 1880s. It was his namesake who was to prove that differentials could be changed.

So how has the M.H. Thatcher government achieved it? The tax system has had an indirect effect. The cuts in tax on high salaries made it cheaper for companies to provide the same amount of take-home pay to more high-paid employees — until the rise in employers' National Insurance in 1985. But while you can use the tax system to give handouts to the rich, it's no longer the fashionable instrument for taking tributes from the poor. The mechanism for *that* is the free market, where the foul takes place on the referee's blind side and looks unintentional.

Although the government policies which were mostly responsible for causing mass unemployment weren't publicly intended to force low incomes on the poor (let alone low incomes paid by the state), the government *is* now explicitly trying to force low earned incomes on the poor, in order to "price them back into jobs" — jobs they had been priced out of by high and volatile interest rates which were simultaneously forcing high incomes on bankers and foreign exchange traders.

Underpaying the underclass

The Tory response to the economic calamity mostly of their own making was state intervention in the labour market to try to depress low wages. Partly this was overt, to "price workers into jobs" under the Jobstart and New Workers schemes and the abolition of Wages Councils, but partly it was at one remove through privatisation of NHS and local council services.

The Jobstart scheme was launched in July 1986, and provides a £20-a-week subsidy to people who've been unemployed for a year if they take a job paying less than £80 a week. Ironically, £80 a week was the figure provisionally put forward by the Trades Union Congress the following month as the legal minimum wage to be brought in by a Labour government. At the same time the government updated the Young Workers Scheme, now called the New Workers Scheme, which provides a £15-a-week subsidy *to the employer* of young people taken on at £55 a week or less (eighteen and nineteen-year-olds) or £65 or less (twenty-year-olds).

It's hardly surprising, then, that over a third of employers visited by the Wages Inspectorate in 1985 were found to be breaking the law by underpaying workers covered by Wages Councils. "But we are just trying to price them into jobs," you can hear them innocently protest. The ghetto of illegal underpayment is the North of England, where over half of employers visited were found to be underpaying. Altogether 16,948 workers in 9,064 firms were found to be underpaid by a total of £2.5 million, but only £1.75 million was recovered. And only two prosecutions were brought against employers.

There are 120 Wages Inspectors, who were able to visit 7 per cent of registered companies in 1985 — at which rate they could expect a visit once every fourteen years. As Tory MP Roger Freeman says, "it is important that the Inspectorate should have not only sufficient numbers, but the organisation and determination to make sure the law is properly enforced" (*Hansard*, 15 May 1986). The government agreed and cut the Inspectorate to seventy-one — after all, it was reducing the scope of Wages Councils, so inspectors would have less to enforce. At the same time, the government announced an increase in the number of social security fraud inspectors from 2,400 to 3,000. The Low Pay Unit commented: "The poor now know that the law will be used against them if they are unemployed but it will not be used to protect them when they are in work."[5]

But, after all these years, there's no evidence that these measures have had any significant effect on job-creation. Unpublished Department of Employment figures obtained by the Low Pay Unit reveal that the government's own surveys show that eight out of ten Young Workers Scheme jobs would have existed anyway: the employers were simply £15 a week better off for each job.

Nevertheless, the government must be given credit for measures which have made incomes more equal. There is one. In 1984 the Chancellor abolished tax relief on life assurance premiums, which tended to be taken up by the better off. There were several other measures that were praiseworthy attempts to show a caring face, but

they are all disqualified on closer examination. The Tories introduced the £10 pensioners' Christmas bonus, for instance, but it was
inadequate compensation for breaking the link with average earnings (which have risen much faster than the Retail Prices Index,
which is what pensions are now linked to).

Some of the changes to income tax rates and thresholds have been
redistributive, but the overall effect of all of them since 1979, taking
inflation and especially National Insurance contributions into
account, has been sharply to increase the after-tax income of the very
rich and to increase the tax burden on everyone else.

In the 1985 Budget, Chancellor Nigel Lawson abolished the ceiling
on employers' National Insurance contributions. This meant that
the employers of those who earned more than £265 a week (£13,780
a year) have to pay an extra 10.45 per cent tax on anything above that
amount. Much to be welcomed, but it hardly qualifies as a whole-
heartedly equalising measure.

Various tax loopholes have been closed, but this is merely the
Inland Revenue's routine firefighting task, and the government has
opened up several new ones by offering new allowances and reliefs.
The Business Expansion Scheme, for example, allows you to save
income tax on investments in new or small businesses, which only
encouraged the setting up of all sorts of companies with risk-free
assets in property or vintage wines.

Supplementary Benefit rates have been increased by more than
inflation (see previous chapter), but they have lagged behind the rise
in average earnings, which have been rising faster still, hence
widening the gap. The Supplementary Benefit rates for people with
children have been increased rather more, but have to be offset by a
rise from 880,000 to 1.6 million in the numbers of children in
families dependent on Supplementary Benefit between 1979 and
1983.[6]

The globalisation of the British economy
Resolute class government is not the sole cause of widening
differentials since 1979. Opening up the British economy to international capital flows — itself partly a result of government policy of
economic *laissez faire* — has also imported the inequalities of the
world economy. The suspension of exchange controls in 1979
helped this process along, but world capital and currency markets
could already decide the policies of individual countries, as the
Labour government's humbling before the imperial court of the

International Monetary Fund in 1976 demonstrated, in a rather crude way.

The most visible forms of this "globalisation" are the rise of London as a centre in a world capital market, associated with the "Big Bang" on the London Stock Exchange in October 1986, and the growing number of conglomerates or holding companies, like Hanson Trust, with substantial overseas interests — especially in the United States.

Britain is becoming a service economy, and there are two kinds of services: financial and labour. Not surprisingly, the differential between the two kinds of employment is greater than the traditional one between management and workers in the manufacturing sector, parts of which no longer exist. Hence banks and brokers compete with other financial centres — New York, Tokyo, Hong Kong — while unskilled manual workers have to compete with Third World sweated labour.

The leading role of the finance sector in pay inequality is confirmed by the Charterhouse survey of top pay in 1,200 companies. There were 688 directors and employees earning more than £100,000 on the Charterhouse database in 1986; 326 of them in industrial and commercial companies, and 362 in financial companies — 216 of these in merchant banks alone. The finance sector has always had high pay levels, but in the past only those who'd served an extended apprenticeship gained access to skyscraper salaries. The media gloss on the new young rich was politically embarrassing, and Mrs Thatcher tried to distance herself from the phenomenon in tones of innocent wonder, just after she and Denis had bought a £350,000 house in Dulwich: "You take salaries in the City, they do make me gasp, two or three hundred thousand pounds so many of them . . . ." (*Newsnight*, BBC television, 30 July 1985).

The process of globalisation has pushed up earnings for all Britain's managers of capital — company bosses as much as City dealers. Suited men in panelled boardrooms have always justified paying themselves ten, twenty, thirty times as much as people they employ on the grounds that "executive remuneration levels" in the United States are a few times higher still. The chronic shortage of supposed managerial talent was illustrated in 1986 by the importation from the United States of Britain's top-paid resident company director, Bob Bauman of Beecham, at an American salary — $1 million, or £690,000 when he took office. But this is occurring not so much because managers of capital are internationally mobile, but because the *capital* is mobile, and the rewards that go with the management of capital are related to the size of capital assets or flows, not to local (that is, British) salary levels.

In 1985, British companies spent more on buying United States companies than Americans spent on acquisitions in the UK. And takeovers, by making companies bigger, increase the rewards of top managers, because companies are blocks of capital assets on which they are paid to earn the best return. To the (as yet limited) extent that managers' pay is a share of profits, gladly paid by grateful shareholders, then it will be determined by the size of the company rather than the structure of differentials within the company, or notions of "the rate for the job".

The 1985–86 phase of British merger mania saw some classic examples of the direct effects of takeovers. Stanley Kalms, after his company Dixons took over Currys, more than doubled his salary to £487,654. His dividends increased to nearly a quarter of a million and he was granted new share options potentially worth at least another half-million if Dixons' shares return to recent levels. His vice-chair Egon von Greyerz and managing director Mark Souhami more than tripled their salaries to between £290,000 and £295,000. Meanwhile at Guinness, chief executive Ernest Saunders controversially increased his salary by 80 per cent to £350,000 after taking over Distillers scotch whisky company (later also controversial, and eventually for Saunders terminally so).

Takeovers and mergers often involve "rationalising" UK operations — meaning job losses — and acquiring and developing companies abroad. A company called BSR International is a striking example of this process. It started as Birmingham Sound Recordings Ltd, and became a West Midlands-based electricals conglomerate centred on one product, the record-changer — the mechanism that lets you play one record after another automatically. Japanese competition had nearly destroyed the company by 1982, despite its branching out into Swan kettles and Goblin teasmades. Almost the only viable part of the business was a Hong Kong-based company called Astec, which made computer circuit boards and which had been bought in 1971. Astec's founders, Australian Brian Christopher and New Zealander Neal Stewart, had been paid in the form of BSR shares and, when BSR looked about to go under, staged a boardroom coup to protect their investments. They enlisted "Dollar Bill" Wyllie, a self-made Australian millionaire, as BSR's new chairperson, and arranged a £50 million rescue plan in the City.

BSR, now BSR International, built on Astec's computer supplies to cash in on the electronics boom. By 1984, two-thirds of its employees were in Hong Kong and Taiwan, half its sales were in the United States and 90 per cent of its profits came from electronics. The company's head office is in Hong Kong, although it's still registered in Wollaston, Stourbridge. And while the company was being transformed into an electronics multinational located only for tax reasons in the UK, thousands of West Midlands jobs were lost, and replaced by cheap labour in the Far East. The new management trio — all resident in Hong Kong — received salaries of £526,000, £526,000 and £145,000 in 1984 (although they all took a big pay cut in 1985, when the downturn in the electronics market worldwide pushed BSR International back into the red again). BSR is a graphic case study in the international forces operating on British manufacturing industry. But on a smaller scale, at the level of each company, the spread of bonus payments to managers and skilled workers has also had the effect of stretching out pay differentials. Mass unemployment is frequently blamed on "rigidities" in the labour market by Conservatives, but the evidence of pay differentials suggest that lower-paid and unskilled workers have responded to market forces by accepting lower pay, while "rigidities" protect managers and high-paid employees, who are able to bid up their performance-related perks.

I'd speculate that the causes of these rigidities are deep-rooted, to do with British education and training and the sociology of firms. They have enabled the benefits of the steep rise in company profits since 1980 to be restricted to those at or near the top of individual firms' hierarchies — and the higher up you are the more you get.

The causes of wealth inequality

"I read recently of one man's vision of wider
property ownership, of a society in which the
British family would be worth £100,000. It looks
like a target out of our reach. But then so would
widespread home ownership and share
ownership have seemed to our parents." —
paragraph Mrs Thatcher dropped from a speech,
Sun, 13 December 1986.

Where the Thatcher government can more plausibly claim to be egalitarian is in the ownership of wealth — even if its period in office is the only one since the First World War when the distribution of wealth has not become more equal. While the Tory party is openly committed to income inequality in the form of "incentive for enterprise", its rhetoric is at the same time strongly framed in terms of a more equal distribution of wealth; notably of home and share ownership. In the case of home ownership the outcome is contra- dictory as, under the rhetoric of spreading wealth, the shape of inequality has changed. The spread of home ownership to a further 6 per cent of the middle-income population might be described as "divisive egalitarianism". It reduces the statistical measure of in- equality, but at the cost of further entombing those excluded by the property franchise from the Tories' democracy — especially council tenants, who constitute most of the poor who are getting poorer in income terms. Local council housing stocks have been cut and house prices are rising. But even if the Conservatives can claim some increase in equality in home ownership, all incentives for wider share ownership have turned out simply to be extra perks for those already on high and secure incomes.

To assess the Conservative record on wealth distribution, we need to understand what causes the shares of wealth owned by different groups to change. So why did the share owned by the richest 1 per cent fall from three-fifths in the 1920s to one-fifth in 1979?

One of the more important explanations is the spread of home ownership, which has boosted the share owned by the 45 per cent below the top 5 per cent, in a mirror image of the top 1 per cent's fall, from one-fifth to three-fifths. Around 1910, in the last years of the "old regime", about 10 per cent of households were owner-occupied and ownership of the remaining rented housing was concentrated in (a few) private hands. The 1930s saw the first great build-up of home- ownership, which accounted for about 30 per cent of households by the Second World War. Growth paused for ten years before resum- ing in the 1950s, rising to 43 per cent in 1960, and then to 50 per cent in 1970, and 55 per cent in 1979.

That doesn't account for all of the shift from the richest 1 per cent within the top half. What has also been happening is a gradual change in the pattern of family ownership and inheritance. In the 1920s, a family's wealth was concentrated in the hands of the oldest male, and the tradition of primogeniture — the passing on of family wealth intact down the male line — was very strong. Although wealth is regarded as shared between spouses in the statistics, adult children in rich families in the 1920s don't show up as wealth owners in their own right. Wealth is now spread more widely in rich families and frequently passed on during the parent's lifetime. Action to avoid estate duty has had a much more equalising effect than the actual amount of tax taken from the rich. Over time, primogeniture has become less rigid — although it is still dominant among the rich — and large wealth-holdings have been broken up. Professor Tony Atkinson argued in *Unequal Shares* that the decline in inequality among the richer half of the population

> reflects in part the rearrangement of wealth within families rather than redistribution between rich and poor families. Although transfers from older to younger members of rich families may represent some diminution of inequality, this is not what most people have in mind when they refer to redistribution (p. 24).

According to more recent research by Professor Tony Shorrocks of Essex University, this process is still going on, as the popularity of trusts as a "tax efficient" way of holding family wealth suggests. But it is a gradual process, and accounts for only about a tenth of the trend towards greater equality in the thirteen years before 1979.

So why haven't the rich increased their share of wealth since 1979? The first point to realise is the momentous nature of the change in 1979. Before then, the apparently gentle drift towards — or at least in the general direction of — equality was inexorable. Over shorter periods than five years, quite sharp shifts between groups could appear to occur, but the longer-term trend towards greater equality always marched on. That trend has been decisively halted.

The equalising factors are still operating, so for the statistics to show a level trend means that the Thatcher government has launched countervailing forces which are concentrating wealth. The old rich are still dissipating their wealth, partly within wider families, and the new home-owners are still adding to the wealth of those who used not to have significant assets at all.

It takes a huge enrichment of the new rich to counterbalance these forces, especially since 1981, when total real personal wealth has been increasing sharply.

The complexity of the undercurrents is illustrated by the two sharp shifts in the distribution of wealth that appeared to happen in the last twenty years (see Table 4, p. 58). During the Heath government, not recognised at the time as a pioneering socialist administration, the share of the top 1 per cent was reduced from 31

TABLE 4

Changes in the Distribution of Wealth 1966–79

Percentage share of

	1966	1971	1974	1979
Top 1%	33	31	23	22
Next 1%	9	8	7	6
Top 5%	56	52	43	40
Next 5%	13	13	14	14
Top 25%	87	86	84	77
Next 25%	10	11	9	18
Bottom 50%	3	3	7	5

Adult population, personal wealth including house, excluding pension rights, UK.

Source: *Inland Revenue Statistics 1978 to 1984.*

per cent to 23 per cent between 1971 and 1974. And during the 1974–79 Labour government the second-richest quarter saw its share of total wealth double from 9 to 18 per cent.[7]

These events aren't a complete mystery. The biggest single form of personal wealth is houses, making up about 40 per cent of the total, and accounting for the vast majority of the wealth of the non-rich. But for millionaires, the most important form of wealth is stocks and shares. So relative changes in house prices and share prices have a direct effect on the relative shares of the top 1 per cent and the rest of the top half. Short-term price fluctuations can have quite dramatic effects on the value of wealth holdings without really changing the distribution of ownership.

Research by Tony Atkinson and Alan Harrison has shown that the share of the top 1 per cent bears a statistical relationship to share prices.[8] Mrs Thatcher's attempt to create a share-owning democracy hasn't affected most of the population, and it's not always appreciated just how concentrated share ownership actually is. In 1981, the Inland Revenue estimates that the top 1 per cent (400,000 individuals) owned three-quarters by value of all the shares in private hands. Chancellor Nigel Lawson's boast that 20 per cent of adults now own shares shouldn't distract us from the fact that valuable holdings are still over-whelmingly concentrated among the richest 1 per cent.

In 1971 Tory Chancellor Anthony Barber's famous "Barber Boom" in the stock market began, holding up the share of the top 1 per cent. At the end of 1973 and throughout 1974 there was a dramatic collapse in share prices to less than half their peak value. Meanwhile 1972 and 1973 saw the biggest house prices surge since the war. Prices fell back (in real terms) in 1974, but they were still 36 per cent higher in real terms than in 1971. So the value of the wealth of the top 1 per cent in relation to that of the rest of the top half of the population fell.

What happened under the Labour government is less clear-cut. The stock market recovered quickly from the 1974 slump, but it didn't get back to 1971 levels in real terms until around 1983. And in 1979 houses in general, although still worth more than before the 1972–73 boom, were worth on average 10 per cent less in real terms than in 1974. Hence there was no dramatic change in the shares of the top 1 per cent and the rest of the top half. But house-price changes in the 1970s, as now, were very uneven, and average prices conceal sharp regional variations. While the richer London and the South East raced ahead in the 1972–73 boom, before falling sharply back, the rest of the country took things at a more sedate pace, and so between 1974 and 1979 prices in Northern Ireland, Scotland and the North of England "caught up" — which may explain part of the rise of the second quarter's share.

This was also a period of high inflation, which eats away at mortgages while boosting the sell-up value of houses, a factor particularly favouring less wealthy home-owners. By 1983, of the £425,000 million-worth of homes owned, only £91,000 million was encumbered by mortgage debt, a historically low level.[9]

So, can the relationship between share and house prices explain the static shares held by percentage groups since 1979? Share prices fell in the 1980 recession but in 1981 began the long steep rise which lasted until the time of writing. Between 1979 and 1984 they rose by 29 per cent in real terms, while average house prices fell by 8 per cent. If anything, this should have sustained the share of wealth owned by the top 1 per cent.[10] But Tony Shorrocks's analysis shows that the effect is surprisingly small. His projection of the Inland Revenue estimates to 1986 suggests that although share prices rose by about a half — in real terms — between 1983 and the peak in April 1986, this would have raised the share of the top 1 per cent by just 1 percentage point.

But, as was previewed in Chapter 4, there is an optical illusion in these figures, caused by the fact that total personal wealth in Britain has been growing fast since 1981. Between 1981 and 1984, for instance, total personal wealth grew by nearly one-fifth in real terms — that is, after allowing for the effect of inflation. After allowing also for the increase in the number of adults, real personal wealth per head increased by a little over one-sixth in those three years.

An increase of one-sixth is worth far more, however, to someone in the top 1 per cent than to someone in the poorer half of the population whose wealth was negligible in the first place. In "Three Nation" terms, the average individual in the top 1 per cent in 1981 was worth £320,000 (in 1984 money), but in 1984 was worth £375,000, a rise of £55,000 after allowing for inflation. The average person in the rest of the richer half of the population was in 1981 worth £22,700 (in 1984 money), and in 1984 was worth £26,600, or £3,900 more. The average wealth-holding in the poorer half was only £1,830 in 1981, and in 1984 was £2,140, a rise of just £310 per head.[11] That small increase was probably overwhelmingly concentrated among the relatively few new home-owners.

Increases of £55,000, £3,900 and £310 are all increases of one-sixth, and hence the wealth ratio between the rich and the poor stays the same, but the amount of money involved in the share owned by the rich is much greater. Individuals in the richest hundredth are still 175 times richer than those in the poorer half, and so have to increase their real wealth massively just to maintain their disproportionately large share of the total. Because wealth is distributed so unequally, information about shares conceals a sharply unequal growth in wealth between 1979 and 1984. The more you've got the more you get.

The mathematical ratio between rich and poor, then, stayed the same between 1979 and, probably, 1986. But the Conservatives make extravagant claims for the equalising effects of their policies. Let's take a critical look at the Tory record on wider home and share ownership.

A property-owning democracy?

"But Hugo, wealth *is* being spread ever more widely — 63 per cent of your fellow countrymen own their own homes," said Ian Gow, then a housing minister, to Hugo Young (*The Thatcher Phenomenon*, BBC Radio 4, 28 May 1985). Not only sexist and selective but also untrue, this is a classic Tory statistic. When he says "men" he means "people", although the figure actually refers to "households", and it's not even the figure for the UK. About 63 per cent of *households* in *England* are owner-occupied. The level of owner-occupation is higher in England than in Scotland (40 per cent) and Northern Ireland (60 per cent), but not Wales (66 per cent).

What matters is not the proportion of houses that are owned by (some of) the people in them, but the proportion of the adult population who are property-owners. No one seems to have done the sums, although the raw survey evidence is available in the government's *General Household Survey*. The reality is that the proportion of the *adult population* owning or part-owning homes has only risen from 50 to 56 per cent.[12] Although the government likes to claim that nearly two in every three Britons share the Tory dream of Wealth Through Bricks, the reality is that it has done little more than reinforce the divide between the wealth owning and the non-wealth-owning halves of the population.

In fact the property owning democracy is doubly false (although not for the council house purchasers), because most of the increase in home ownership is in privatised council houses. For those who don't have council tenancies to buy out at a discount, it's still very difficult to buy a home. As Michael Heseltine, then the minister responsible for housing, pointed out after Mrs Thatcher came to power: "To subsidise mortgage rates would simply encourage house price increase, and switch the burden from those who have just bought to those who are saving up to buy" (26 November 1979). Since this warning was given there has been no evidence that the ratio between income and house price has got worse for first-time buyers, except in London. But houses are more expensive than they would be without mortgage tax relief.

The drive towards increasing home ownership is petering out. The Nationwide building society predicted that the market was "close to saturation point" in July 1986, and it estimated that 30 per cent of households "cannot realistically expect" to buy. Council house sales, at their peak of 222,000 in 1982, fell to 109,000 in 1985.

House prices in general have risen since 1984 but very unequally, with spectacular rises in London and the South East balanced by rises below the rate of inflation in the North and outside England. Put hypothetically, if you bought two houses for the same amount, say a Chelsea flat and a Northern country house for £100,000 in 1979, the flat was worth £210,000 in 1986, whereas the country house was worth only £165,000. A £100,000 stately home in Northern Ireland would have been worth just £139,000.[13] This is likely to have the effect of increasing the share of wealth owned by the richest 10 per cent of the population.

Although more unequal incomes have a direct effect through saving on wealth holdings, they also affect the distribution of wealth through house prices. Partly because building societies and banks lend on multiples of earnings, there is quite a close correlation between earnings and house prices, so growing income inequality can lead straight into a greater concentration of wealth. The upwards escalation of house prices in London reflects the top pay explosion in business head offices and financial and professional services, and translates it into more unequal wealth holdings.

"As everybody knows, the only way to live in London and the South East is to have a house there already," the *Sun* pointed out on 5 March 1986. But what's the cause of this great regional disparity? The *Sun* has the answer, from Professor (of Modern History) John Vincent:

> It all starts with sky-high land prices. Yet the so-called shortage of building land is a delusion. The bad habits of nationalised industries are much to blame. They always hang on to derelict land just in case it might come in handy.

Yes, well, let us move on.

When the *Financial Times* conducted a survey of the £100,000 price contour (31 May 1986), the closest it could get to central London for houses was the rapidly gentrifying East End, although it was still possible to get a small one-bedroom flat in central London for under six figures. The *Financial Times* reported that the "six-figure price wave" was moving out of London and down the main commuter routes at great speed. An Ipswich estate agent explained why people were queuing up to pay £225,000 for a six-bedroom country manor: it's all these "young people in the City on high salaries and with golden hellos to spend". But "sever connections with London altogether", the *Financial Times* reporter found, "and house prices take on a totally different complexion." An estate agent in Accrington, Lancashire, reported forlornly: "I do have terraced houses on the books for £5,000 to £5,500. The difficulty is finding something as expensive as £100,000."

In less obvious ways, too, property is starting to function as a mechanism for preserving and perpetuating wealth inequalities, rather than spreading wealth more widely. The children of those who became home owners in the first growth period, the 1930s, are now inheriting the locked-up wealth of their parents. Their parents, say in their thirties when they were first-time buyers before the war, are now dying off, passing on property, unencumbered by a mortgage, to children who often already own their own homes. The "class" division by housing tenure means that the children of home owners are overwhelmingly home owners themselves. Almost all (93 per cent) of owner-occupied households where the householder is over sixty-five are owned outright, and these about-to-be-inherited assets make up 21 per cent of all owner-occupied households.[14] This, too, can be expected to increase the wealth share of the richest 10 per cent or so. So if the Tory property-owning democracy is limited to a narrower franchise than you might have thought, and home owner-ship looks like a factor that is now responsible for *concentrating* wealth in certain geographical areas, what about this shareholder democracy we hear so much about?

A share-owning democracy?
"Every man a capitalist," declares Mrs Thatcher generously, whenever the interview seems to be flagging. And, she says, verbally grabbing her questioner by the lapels, "what's wrong with that?"

If the government were proposing to share out all personal capital in Britain equally among its citizens, most of them, obtaining £32,000 (in 1987), wouldn't find anything wrong with it.[15]

Unfortunately, though, this is a government that lives in the real world. It doesn't have money to "give away". What Mrs Thatcher would like is wider property ownership and wider share ownership, but not of course at the expense of those who already own these liberating commodities. What Conservatives would like, when they advocate employee share ownership, is that workers should have capital *instead* of wages. And why? Partly so that workers will get less if profits are low, but also to provide incentives in a way which weakens their collective loyalties to each other and to other workers.

Wider share ownership is now a vogue concept with all three political parties, but their motives are different. The Tories would like to see wages "downwardly adjustable"; the Liberal/SDP Alliance would like people to be nicer to each other, workers and employers having a tendency to fight in the playground; and the Labour Party would like an element of worker control and participation. All three would like "wealth to be spread more widely", but for all three this appears to mean that everybody should be better off.

The Tory vision of democracy is a "shareholder democracy", which started life as property-owning democracy, literally, in the days when you had to have property to vote. To Conservatives, voting is a dangerous thing only to be entrusted to responsible people. Hence Norman Tebbit's claim that local council elections are "distorted" by people who are allowed to vote even though they don't pay rates. Hence also the plan to cut rate rebates so that everyone should pay a fifth of their rates, no matter how poor they are. The next stage would be to allow people to claim the full rebate as long as they agree not to vote.

The trouble with the share-owning democracy is that shares aren't a particularly good investment, because they don't have the tax advantages of houses or pension funds (which invest in shares on your behalf). You have to pay income tax on your dividends and Capital Gains Tax on their rise in price, and you can't deduct investments from your taxable income like mortgage interest payments and pension contributions. In some ways, the shares of your own company are the worst investment. If your employer went bust, not only would you lose your job but your investment too. America has seen the rapid spread of employee share ownership — but only because of tax subsidies which are more generous than in Britain, the result of a campaign prefigured by Louis Kelso's *The Capitalist Manifesto* in 1958, and taken up in the mid – 1970s by senator Russell Long, son of the populist Louisiana politician Huey Long.

David Howell, former Energy and Transport Minister, expounds the virtues of wider share ownership in an aptly-named book called *Blind Victory* (1986). His argument is that unemployment is caused because starting wages are too high (although unemployment, he says, is part of oldthink, and unemployment figures are based on a "misleading and outdated definition of work"). However, he disagrees with callous "classical economists [who] argue that a low wage is better than no wage". Luckily there is a way to transcend this brutalism, and Howell calls it "softnomics" (sic):

> It is to seek to compensate, as far as possible, through capital distribution, for what the employment market mechanism can no longer provide through conventional wages and salaries. It is to allow the market for wages to work while encouraging genuine equality of status and circumstance through widespread personal capital accumulation (p. 122).

Let me phrase it better for him: "If the unemployed had some income from capital, they'd accept lower wages and everyone would have work." But how and why and by whom should *capital* be allocated to the unemployed and the low-paid when *income* isn't?

I asked Nigel Forman MP this question. He's one of David Howell's wet supporters, who thinks wider capital ownership is a good way of conning Thatcherites into a more egalitarian politics (I paraphrase). "But that is assuming a static model," he protested. But isn't all the evidence that the distribution of income and wealth *is* static, and if not static moving in the direction of greater inequality? But individuals, he says, are more likely these days to go through periods of high, medium and low earnings. Short-term contracts are becoming more common. "And the poor old working class, what's left of it, is quite used to working on or off the lump." So, greater inequality is illusory. It's just that people are sometimes rich and sometimes poor, so that at any one moment they may appear to be unequal, but in a couple of years' time they'll all have changed round.

Social mobility in Britain *has* increased since the war, but the rate of "turnover" is too slow to compensate for the greater inequality under Thatcherism. In any case, mobility is still highly selective, whereas the Howell-Forman thesis requires the whole of the working class to be recycled through prosperous periods, so that they can earn enough in short spurts to accumulate the capital that will see them through leaner times.

National Freight Consortium plc

There aren't many examples of "people's capitalism" around, so the one that always gets wheeled out is the National Freight Consortium. The NFC was bought by its workers in 1982. The state-owned parcels operation was the only concern named in the 1979 Conservative manifesto for privatisation, but ran into financial trouble and was only just sold off in time for the 1983 election, for a mere £5 million.

Ministers still regard it as a jewel in the crown of the privatisation programme because 83 per cent of its shares are held by employees, former employees and their families. But the reason why such a high proportion of employees hold shares is that share ownership is restricted to employees, former employees and their families by the terms of the buy-out (the "Share Family"). No one else, apart from the group of banks who financed the buy-out, and who hold the other 17 per cent, is *allowed* to own the shares. Only three-fifths of the employees own shares, and most of those are holdings worth under £10,000. On the other hand, four of the directors have holdings worth over £1 million, at the last valuation in 1986. Sir Peter Thompson, the chairperson who organised what was in effect a familiar "management buy-out" with better employee benefits in 1982, got 40,000 shares which are now worth as much as £1,250,000.

NFC is no more an example of "people's capitalism" than the John Lewis Partnership is a co-op; it's a more benevolent form of capitalist company, a bit like Marks and Spencer. Despite all the fine phrases about a "share-owning democracy" the result of the NFC experiment, like the Conservatives' share-ownership legislation, is a bigger profit for those who are at the top anyway.

Share options: your pound in their pocket

The government's priorities are perfectly illustrated by the generous tax relief granted to executive share option schemes, which are typically worth hundreds of thousands of pounds, as compared with the "modest" tax benefits available to what are known as ordinary "employee share schemes", where the tax relief is limited to the profit that can be made on £6,000-worth of shares over five years.

Share option schemes work by granting the option to employees to buy the company's shares at a certain price, usually the share price at the time the options were granted. As the share price rises, the right to buy shares at the old price becomes more and more valuable. This profit can easily be cashed in by reselling the shares on the stock market as soon as the option is exercised. To take a simple example: Dick Giordano, until recently recipient of the highest salary paid by a British company — £883,100 in 1985. In 1982 he was granted the option to buy 400,000 shares in BOC, of which he is chairperson and chief executive, at a price of £2 a share. He can exercise his options between 1986 and 1989, but BOC shares have recently been up to £4.71, at which price Giordano would make a profit of £2.71 a share, or £1,084,000.

BOC is an unusual case. Few other companies whose directors stand to gain such amounts provide such clear information. The value of an individual's share options does not have to be disclosed in company accounts. The Companies Act requires only that the number of shares in which directors are "interested" be published. Unlike in the United States, no information is given in the accounts about the profits directors actually make when they take up their options. Directors' share sales do have to be declared to the Stock Exchange, however, and are published in its *Weekly Official*

Intelligence (which does not have an index: in many cases it will be impossible to work out how much money they've made without regular scrutiny of *Weekly Official Intelligence* and several years' company accounts).

Directors are only beginning to cash in their subsidised gains, as the tax relief, introduced in August 1984, can't be taken up for three years (unless there's a takeover). But tax relief on share options was only brought in after a battle within the government.

In January 1983, junior Treasury minister Nicholas Ridley explained why the government wouldn't give in to pressure to bring in subsidies for executive share option:

> Many people are urging us to re-introduce the 1972 share option scheme for key executives. One is torn here in two directions. First the incentive effect of these schemes on top managers undoubtedly had considerable effect, although how much is not provable. Second, and opposite, there is a clear unfairness about schemes which can bring large benefits to the lucky few selected by the Chairman, in which others in the same enterprise cannot participate. And furthermore it is a one-way bet!

But, he went on, "we continue to search for ways forward that can give the incentive effect for top managers, without discriminating against those of whom the poet says 'they also serve who only stand and wait'." Only a year later, his government decided to discriminate against them after all.

This is the bookie state with a vengeance: the low-paid are encouraged to buy personal pensions dependent on the Hidden Hand of the stock market (government warning: "your investment may go down as well as up"), while top managers are subsidised on their "one-way bets".

The one-way bet description is endorsed by Harold Geneen, former chief executive of American electronics giant ITT, who says caustically: "When the stock market goes up, everyone cashes in — when it goes down the board issues new options at lower prices" (*Fortune* magazine, September 1984).

But Ridley's successor John Moore was keen. Ridley and Moore are both leading figures on the free-market Right, but they differed on tactics: Ridley stuck to his principles and rejected the coverage of the proposed relief as élitist and distorting the free market. For Moore the end — capital incentives for managers — would justify the tax subsidy means.

The tax relief on executive share options is also opposed by the Wider Share Ownership Council (a mainly Tory pressure group) because it fears that it will have, "as in the early 1970s, the effect of conferring special benefits on senior management in which the wider workforce did not participate".[16] Several back-bench Tory MPs agree. "The great thing in life is to encourage everybody, not just the few," says Anthony Beaumont-Dark. "Capitalism has to be seen to be fair." Nigel Forman, who tried and failed to amend the 1986 Finance Bill to force companies with executive share option schemes to provide some form of scheme for all employees, says he doesn't agree with those "hardliners in the Tory party who think that whatever's good for managers is good for everyone else".

Sir Christopher Hogg, chairperson of Courtaulds, praises share option schemes: "Anything which can lead everybody in a company to see that they have a common interest in the success of that company is worth promoting."[17] His share option scheme was worth around half a million pounds to him at the time. Ordinary Courtaulds employees are not eligible for the scheme. The tax relief on the "Save As You Earn" option scheme they can join is limited to the profit that can be made on £6,000-worth of shares. Indeed John Moore cajoled the Institute of Directors in December 1984:

> I should remind you that the new approved share option schemes need not benefit only executives or the highest paid staff. Companies can use these schemes to benefit all or any of their workforce — not directors or executives only.

His plea went unheeded in the headlong rush to register new schemes with the Inland Revenue. Over 1,500 companies have registered. Over 61 per cent of all companies covered in Charterhouse's annual pay and perks survey had executive share options by August 1986. Only one scheme that I have come across so far, the *Independent*'s, is open to all employees. Only 35 per cent had Save As You Earn schemes for ordinary employees.

"When I first entered parliament in 1974," John Moore went on, "achieving a people's capital market in my lifetime as a politician seemed an impossible dream." It still is. Contrast the political daydream of a lean, fit economy bursting with the vitality of an enterprise culture with the reality of the morass of legal controls and tax rules of mind-boggling complexity on a perk like share options. But John Moore was carried away by his own rhetoric.

If wealth and ownership can be spread, it is possible to break down those illusory barriers between "them" and "us", between employers and employees, between management and workers that have been the bane of British society and the undermining of British economic life. Our aim is to consign to the dustbin that most misleading of phrases "the two sides of industry" that has done untold damage to Britain.

If the barriers are illusory, why do they have to be broken down?

There is no better way to promote a sense of "them" and "us" than this government's "incentive" policy of giving tax reliefs worth hundreds of thousands of pounds to encourage share option schemes that can produce profits of millions (see Table 8, p. 139) for a tiny minority of board directors and senior managers. Meanwhile British Telecom's latest accounts (1986) show that 1.2 million of the 1.5 million individual shareholders have holdings of fewer than 800 shares, worth less than £1,500, and own just 7.3 per cent of the company.

Setting my people free

So the notion of a nation of capital owners is a sham. But some Conservative legislation might have had unexpected effects in the direction of equalising wealth. Many of the government's tax reductions on capital have had the perverse effect of reducing concentrations of wealth by giving existing wealth-holders more incentive to spend some of it.

In particular the top rate of income tax, which was 83 per cent, combined with the unearned income surcharge of 15 per cent, produced a tax rate of 98 per cent on interest and dividends from investments and locked up a lot of capital, because people preferred investments which didn't produce income. This capital was easier to release when the top combined rate came down to 75 per cent (60 + 15 per cent) in 1979 and the thresholds were raised. The lower rates of income tax made it much more worthwhile to business owners to pay themselves large salaries, instead of keeping all their wealth tied up in the business. The Capital Gains Tax threshold was raised and the Capital Transfer Tax threshold was also doubled from £25,000 to £50,000 in 1980. (The higher-rate Capital Transfer Tax bands were also generously increased in 1982 — the threshold for the 60 per cent rate, for example, going up from £160,000 to £250,000.)

There have been more wealth-liberating tax laws which might

affect the distribution of wealth since 1984, the last year for which Inland Revenue estimates are published. In 1984 the unearned income surcharge was abolished, meaning wealth-owners pay less tax on their interest, dividends and rent than on salaries (which attract National Insurance contributions). In 1985, capital gains that had accumulated since 1982 because of inflation were released from tax (only the real gain is now taxed). In 1986, lifetime Capital Transfer Tax was abolished, allowing completely tax-free transfers seven years or more before death. All these measures make it easier for wealth holdings to be realised, without paying tax, and spent on high living, or on consumer goods which don't keep their value, or to be spread more widely within families, enhancing the "Atkinson effect" (described on p. 57).

---

1. Figures for average tax rates are for a married man with £2,000 of tax allowances on top of his personal allowance, from John Kay and Mervyn King, *The British Tax System* (Oxford University Press, second edition, 1980, p. 28). For someone on a salary of £30,000, worth £52,000 in 1986, the tax boost was from £15,000 after tax to £18,000, up 25 per cent.

2. The £3,600 million figure is derived by Doug Jones, economic adviser to Roy Hattersley, from various parliamentary answers, and is used as the basis for the Labour Party's tax planning. The £15,000 tax cut figure is derived from parliamentary answers by Harry Cohen MP (press release 11 August 1986), and the savings on the social security budget by Michael Meacher MP.

3. Inland Revenue note (1982) to the Meacher Committee (Treasury and Civil Service Committee, Third Special Report 1982–83 session, "The Structure of Personal Income Taxation and Income Support", HMSO May 1983, HC-386, 20-II, Appendices p. 158).

4. John Donaldson and Pamela Philby (eds.), *Pay Differentials*, Gower 1985.

5. Low Pay Unit, *Low Pay Review* 26, summer 1986.

6. There was also a rise, from 290,000 to 400,000, in the numbers of children in families with income below the Supplementary Benefit level. Source: DHSS, "Low Income Families 1983", July 1986.

7. These estimates were not calculated using the latest computer program, which produced or revised the estimates for the years since 1980, and so are not exactly comparable with the figures shown in Table 3.

8. A.B. Atkinson and A.J. Harrison, *The Distribution of Personal Wealth in Britain*, Cambridge University Press 1978.

9. Financial Statistics annual supplement 1985, HMSO.

10. Selecting the dates 1974, 1979 and 1984 gives the misleading impression of steadily falling real house prices, partly because 1974 was the tail end of the 1972–73 boom, which was much higher in real terms than either that of 1978–79, or the present upward trend which, to date, has been confined to London and the South East. The underlying trend in house prices has been to rise in step with earnings (apart from 1972–74 and 1979–80, average house prices since 1956 have been between 2.9 and 3.5 times average male earnings). Of course, houses are a much better investment than they appear because of the tax-subsidised and inflation-reduced loans to buy them with, the tax-free capital gain, and because home-owners don't pay rent.

11. *Inland Revenue Statistics 1986* (HMSO), Series C wealth, excluding pension rights. Total wealth increased by 19 per cent in real terms between 1981 and 1984, but wealth per head increased by 17 per cent because of the increase in the number of adults in the UK.

12. Assuming that where a married man is described as "head of household" that his wife also owns a share — the proportion of couples who draw up a legal agreement to specify the contrary must be statistically insignificant — 56 per cent of the over-eighteen population in Great Britain were owner-occupiers in 1986. The figure derived from the General Household Survey for 1983 is 52.5 per cent, but the survey underrecords home ownership by about 2 percentage points if compared with the 1981 Census (see Note 1 to chapter 6 "Tenure", *General Household Survey 1983*, MHSO), and there has also been a rise of up to two percentage points between 1983 and 1986, according to the Building Societies Association.

13. Building Societies Association, *Building Society Fact Book 1986*, average regional house prices.

14. *Building Societies Association Bulletin*, July 1986.

15. *Inland Revenue Statistics 1986* (HMSO): the balance sheet total for personal wealth including private sector pensions was £1,028,000 million in 1984, assuming 10 per cent growth per annum and 42.7 million adults in the UK.

16. Letter to the *Financial Times*, 17 April 1984.

17. Interviewed on London Weekend Television's *Fortune* programme, August 1986.

PART II
WHAT CAN BE DONE

6. IDEOLOGY OF INEQUALITY

> "To convert a phenomenon, however
> interesting, into a principle, however respectable,
> is an error of logic." — R.H. Tawney on
> inequality, *Equality*, 1931, p. 40.

The conclusion of Part I is that inequality has worsened since 1979, and that much of that worsening was a direct result of government policy. How might a government that was committed to reversing that trend and rekindling the long march towards greater equality begin? The first difficulty, of course, is to define what sort of society we would like to see.

The morality of inequality is at the heart of the three modern ideologies of socialism, liberalism and conservatism. Socialism holds that we "ought" to be equal, and hence "ought" to change society to allow people to be as equal as possible. Conservatism holds that it isn't possible and so we "ought" not to try. Liberalism holds that individuals "ought" to be free to be unequal as long as they don't restrict other people's freedom to be unequal too. For conservatives, the prevailing extent of inequality is about right and if the rich become richer that's all right too, and perfectly natural. It's only not all right if the state tries to take away from the rich to give to the poor.

But as long ago and in as different circumstances as those of Plato, the desirability of limiting material inequality was recognised, although Plato stressed the pragmatic reasons of social order rather than morality. He suggested a maximum wealth of between two and four times the minimum.

> It is necessary in a State which is to avoid that greatest of plagues, which is better termed disruption than class discord, that none of its citizens should be in a condition of either painful poverty or wealth; consequently the lawgiver must declare a limit for both these conditions. Having set [the lower] limit, the lawgiver shall

allow a man to possess twice this amount, or three times or four times. Should anyone acquire more than this — whether by discovery or gift or money-making, or through gaining a sum exceeding the due measure by some other such piece of luck — if he makes the surplus over to the State and the gods who keep the State, he shall be well-esteemed and free from penalty.
(*Laws*, Book V.)

It has to be said that even in ancient Greece this was not a profound analysis. It doesn't take into account several very important factors: including age, income, sex and slavery.

However, the multiple of four has a curious resonance, and provides a promising starting point for considering practical limits to inequality in modern society. Applied to income, it suggests the maximum inequality would be, say, between £5,000 a year for an unskilled sixteen-year-old and £20,000 a year for Ralph Halpern, chairperson of Burton (he was the second-highest-paid British employee in 1986, on £1,004,000). "No one should earn more than four times as much as anyone else" is quite an attractive socialist slogan.

This is all very plausible until we try to put into the equation the other factors Plato left out. The multiple of four allows us to take account of income rising with age (although there's no ethical reason why it should), but what about sex? If we say the poorest he or she in England gets £5,000 a year and the richest person isn't allowed more than £20,000 (*after tax*), what if two of the richest kind live together, saving one lot of mortgage payments and only needing one vacuum cleaner? The disposable income of each of the couple (if they share it equally) now exceeds four times that of the poorest single person. And if the poor single person has a child to look after, the differential becomes even greater.

As for slavery, or at least unemployment, do we say the unemployed single person gets £5,000 a year in benefits and the unskilled sixteen-year-old in a job gets £6,000? We begin to understand why Plato passed quickly on to other more pressing subjects. In any case, he wasn't talking about income, he was legislating for inequalities of wealth, and would need a few Platonic statutory instruments in the modern world, because "citizens" for Plato meant men of property. In a modern free society, which is of course what a socialist one would be, you can't stop people *not* owning things. And if citizens are free to get into debt, four times the wealth of someone with net debts is not a useful limit.

Of course unemployment isn't the modern equivalent of slavery: it's the family — combining sex and slavery — that is the central problem of the morality of inequality. And it's the combination of the family, authority and wealth, in the form of "family property", that is for conservatives the best argument and defence against egalitarianism. Robert Nisbet, an American conservative historian, says:

> Much of the conservative veneration for the family lies in the historic affinity between family and property. The medieval laws of primogeniture and entail by which family property could pass intact to the oldest son and could not be alienated from the family line obviously bespoke a high regard for the family as the best possible means of protection against dissipation and fragmentation of property, its centre of gravity almost invariably land. There is no issue over which conservative has fought liberal and socialist as strenuously as on threats through law to loosen property from family grasp, by taxation or by any other form of redistribution (*Conservatism*, p. 52).

Contemporary Toryism is perhaps less feudal and has borrowed more from economic liberalism, but the sacredness of family property is unimpeached; a potent if inconsistent mix of the family and the free market. The justification of greater inequality propounded by today's Thatcherites is the classic economic-liberal doctrine that freedom for entrepreneurs benefits those (for example workers thrown on the dole) who appear at first sight to be less free; or that it benefits them far more in the long run than direct transfers of resources from rich to poor. "You are not doing anything against the poor by seeing the top people are paid well," Mrs Thatcher says. "How else are you going to succeed except through the talent and ability of the most able?" (*Newsnight*, BBC television, 30 July 1985).

The first thing egalitarians have to do is engage with the arguments against equality at a philosophical level. And, at first, liberals appear to be their allies. While economic liberalism has been hijacked by the conservatives, social liberalism seems to have drifted towards the Left. But there is still a very important difference between the status of equality in liberal philosophy (which, more than anything identifiable as social-democratic, lies behind the thinking of the British Liberal/Social Democratic Party Alliance) and its status in socialist philosophy, so it's vital to distinguish between the two approaches.

One of the more important works on modern ethics, *A Theory of Justice* (1971) by American liberal philosopher John Rawls, has been described as egalitarian. It puts forward the "Principle of Difference", by which inequality is judged in terms of the position of the least advantaged member of society. Rawls proposes two basic principles of justice, the first being that every member of a society "has an equal right to the most extensive liberty compatible with a like liberty for all", a principle made famous by John Stuart Mill in *On Liberty* in 1859. The second principle is that all inequalities "are arbitrary unless it is reasonable to expect that they will work out to everyone's advantage". This principle is also found in Mill's work, but he was scathing about egalitarianism:

> It is known that the bad workmen, who form the majority of operatives in many branches of industry, are decidedly of the opinion that bad workmen ought to receive the same wages as good, and that no one ought to be allowed, through piecework or otherwise, to earn by superior skill or industry more than others can without it (*On Liberty*, p. 144).

Nevertheless, Mill also subjected inequality — where it arose through no fault of the citizen — to the requirement that it must serve "social utility" (*Utilitarianism*, p. 54).

Rawls's advance on nineteenth-century utilitarianism was to substitute the welfare of the least well-off for "the greatest good of the greatest number" as the measure of social utility and hence of justice. Despite this step forward, however, Rawls's egalitarianism remains subordinate to the first priority, that of maximising liberty. He relegates the goal of equality to "third division status", according to Professor Keith Dixon. In *Freedom and Equality* (1986), Dixon provides a clear summary — and refreshing critique — of Rawls's monumentally abstruse 600-page book:

> Rawls assumes that there will, of necessity, be differences in the distribution of economic goods and services. Hence he labels his principle of equality the "Principle of Difference". This change of designation is highly significant! Inequalities, according to Rawls's Principle of Difference, can always in principle be justified. The contrary is true, however, for the Principle of Liberty. (p. 55.)

What's more, the Principle of Difference is itself in two parts. To quote Rawls:

Social and economic inequalities are to be arranged so that they are (a) to the greatest benefit of the least advantaged; [and] (b) attached to offices and positions open to all under conditions of fair equality of opportunity (p. 60).

But sub-principle (b), equality of opportunity, takes precedence over sub-principle (a). Returning to Dixon's paraphrase: "It is not permissible, according to Rawls, to improve the lot of the poor if this involves denying or restricting opportunities to other members of society" (p. 57), which rules out positive discrimination, or "affirmative action" as it's called in America.

As long as they are both more or less "free", Rawls regards society X as more "just" if it provides a higher standard of living for its poorest member than society Y, regardless of the fact that Y is more equal. "For Rawls there is nothing wrong with inequality as long as it produces the goods, so to speak, for the lower orders," according to Dixon (p. 58). He claims that genuine egalitarianism, while it may be directed towards remedying the unfair distribution of resources, is more importantly "a recognition of the intrinsic undesirability of hierarchy", and seeks to create a "republic of equals". He argues that socialists are — or ought to be — prepared to make some material sacrifice for the sake of greater equality (and that might be especially true in modern industrialised countries when the ecological costs of constant economic growth are so high). A more equal distribution of fewer resources might be better than greater but unequal affluence for all, even if this made the poorest materially better off.

Evolving ethics

Moving from abstract philosophy to current political struggles, it is the moral values of the free market that are at issue. In the Middle Ages, differentials of income or wealth were thought to be determined by God. But with the decline in theological explanations and the development of labour market flexibility, decisions about the distribution of resources had to be given over to Adam Smith's "hidden hand" of the market in the eighteenth century.

Conservatives often argue that the market is value-free, to try to avoid what they would otherwise accept as moral constraints. The more sophisticated new Right thinkers, however, have given market judgments moral force. The "evolutionary theory of ethics", adumbrated by Friedrich Hayek, is a blend of social Darwinianism, free-market economics and mysticism.

Tradition is in effect not the result of selection of individuals, but of group selection — with the result that the individual can never understand it. Traditional rules of conduct were selected by evolution for effects which the individual could never be aware of (*The Guardian*, 17 September 1984).

So, if you find yourself earning a mere fraction of Professor Hayek's comfortable income, lie back and reflect that the accumulated and ineluctable wisdom of your countrypersons over the ages is that it's much better this way. You may not be able to understand why it should be so, but then you are but one human being, while Professor Hayek has managed to decipher the unconscious decision of countless millions.

The world owes me a living

One victim of market forces, unable to decipher this wisdom, is a solicitor who appeared on a television programme about the end of the conveyancing monopoly ("Scales of Justice", Yorkshire TV, 11 August 1986):

A bit of competition is quite stimulating, but if you have too much it then becomes a destructive force, and it has driven prices down in this area and perhaps nationally as well by 30 or 40 per cent. Times have become quite stringent financially. I still have three children who go to a fee-paying school and they've been there for a number of years, and when they went it was quite in the context of the sort of earnings I had at that time that they should do so. But with the changes, the situation has become really quite different and it — to be open about it — it's much more of a struggle to maintain that basis of education.

It all depends on how much competition is too much. How free is the free market? Sir Gordon White, chairperson of the United States arm of Hanson Trust, a British company engaged in a crusade for its vision of free-market values, believes that monopolies are only bad if they are state-sponsored.

The division of labour has become so specific and so refined that the concept of competition within the UK is meaningless without appreciating the presence of international traders. If markets remain open internationally the monopoly status of one firm will always be fragile and subject to dissolution by innovation or price. Most monopolies depend on some form of collusion or support of state agencies. Monopoly is not the enemy of the general interest, unless it is the downstream result of the state itself. The market is a constant democratic procedure which seeks to replace what's turned out to be incompetent management with what is hoped will be successful management. The government's duty is to get out of the way (*The Guardian*, 17 July 1986).

Nineteenth-century liberals like Jeremy Bentham believed that free trade and the abolition of primogeniture, together with equality before the law and equality of opportunity, would by themselves result in greater material equality.

If the laws do not oppose [equality], if they do not maintain monopolies, if they do not permit entails, large properties will be seen without effort, without revolutions, without shock, to sub-divide themselves by little and little ("Principles of the Civil Code"). [1]

This sort of reasonableness is no match for Conservatism, which is a crude political principle, but a very subtle psychological weapon, as some of the more intellectual Tories have acknowledged. None, however, is so cynical as Maurice Cowling, the Cambridge historian and very much a socialist's right-winger.

In the Conservative conception of freedom there is a great deal of double-talk and many layers of concealed consciousness. Conservatives, if they talk about freedom long enough, begin to believe that that is what they want. But it is not freedom that Conservatives want; what they want is the sort of freedom that will maintain existing inequalities or restore lost ones, so far as political action can do this. And this is wanted not only by those who benefit from inequalities of wealth, rank and education but also by the enormous numbers who, while not partaking in the benefits, recognise that inequalities exist, and in some obscure sense, assume that they ought to. Inequalities are things they associate with a properly functioning society (*Conservative Essays*, 1978, p. 9).

Why, if inequality in Britain is so great, is there not a much greater resentment on the part of the mass of people who have relatively little? Why, in Maurice Cowling's words, do they appear to assume that inequalities ought to exist?

One of the most important theoretical studies of this question was Walter Runciman's *Relative Deprivation and Social Justice* in 1966.

Because he's an Honourable and not a socialist, the Left has neglected his attempt to explain why the Western working class does not ensure the near permanent rule of socialist governments. There seems little choice: either you believe that a wicked capitalist conspiracy has, by manipulating the media, duped the working class into misunderstanding its position in the hierarchy, or you accept Runciman's notion of "limited reference groups" by which disadvantaged groups judge their unequal status.

In every workplace, there's a complex of compartments which obstruct direct comparisons. "Temporary" workers can be paid less than half as much as permanent staff for doing the same job side by side. The "staff" and "manual" ("monthly" and "weekly" in the common euphemism) division is less widespread than it used to be, partly because of bankruptcies among traditional manufacturing concerns. But new distinctions, as between part-timers and full-timers, "core" staff and contract staff continue to allow comparative horizons to be limited. Runciman suggests that wider comparisons are often only made during times of change — such as during the war — because "frustrated expectations are less readily tolerable than consistent hardship".

One of the best practical studies of how limited reference groups work is Duncan Gallie's comparison between the radicalism of British and French workers in 1971−72 (*Social Inequality and Class Radicalism in France and Britain*, 1983). In it he sets out to explain why French workers are consistently more politically radical than British ones, displaying a much greater class resentment against inequality. The explanation does not appear to be because France is a more unequal society: although incomes are more unequally distributed there than in Britain, the distribution of wealth was more equal in France in the 1970s. And in neither case is people's awareness of the extent of inequality precise enough to allow them to compare themselves with the situation in other countries.

The context of Gallie's study is the wide variation in political radicalism of the working class in different European countries as confirmed by a number of opinion polls (Table 5).

In the 1970s, the majority of French manual workers identified themselves in opinion polls as working-class, whereas a majority of British manual workers claimed not to belong to any social class and only 37 per cent volunteered the description of themselves as working-class.[2]

The more detailed questions in Gallie's study of two British and

TABLE 5

Working-Class Radicalism in Europe 1976–79

Manual workers

	UK	France	Italy	W Germany
Reducing inequality between rich and poor: very important	21%	62%	62%	33%
Dissatisfied with the way democracy works	39%	60%	81%	19%
Favour revolution (instead of reform or status quo)	6%	18%	8%	2%

Source: Data from several "Eurobarometers" combined by Gallie to provide samples of between 297 and 1,422 (average of those shown 737).

two French groups of oil refinery workers revealed that French workers were more likely to see society in terms of two classes, and to see themselves as being in the lower one. British workers were more likely to describe themselves as middle-class. This was related to French workers' greater tendency to see class structure in terms of the workplace. Where unprompted British workers tended to describe the highest class as the "upper class", French workers used terms denoting a specifically business élite ("le patronat", "les industriels", "les capitalistes") or the bourgeoisie. (British workers were also more likely to refer to the aristocracy.) This was despite the fact that the French workers interviewed earned considerably more than the regional average, while the British workers were only just above their regional average.

Not only were French workers more aware of inequality and keener to see something done about it, but their sense of inequality was twice as likely to be related to the workplace: saying they were aware of class differences in the way they were treated at work, and so on. British workers were more likely to see inequality "in the way some get the benefit of political decisions", or in social relations or housing.

Although the French Communist Party and communist trade union CGT had a role in shaping or articulating the politics of French workers in Marxist form, this only begs the question, why were French workers more receptive to communism? The main explanations for this are historical, and Gallie traces the different experience of the two world wars in Britain and France. The First World War hit France much harder than Britain, and the working class in France suffered more. But the French working class were far more ready to fight when the war started, because it directly threatened the French nation. Appeals to nationalism were less successful with British workers, and there were strikes by munitions workers on the Clyde and South Wales miners in 1915. As a result, the wartime government of Lloyd George made significant concessions to trade union leaders in return for their supporting the war effort. This meant that the British trade union movement emerged from the war with an enhanced ability to negotiate with employers and state through a developed bargaining system. In France, however, the government responded to industrial unrest after the war by repression and supported employers' coercion. The French Communist Party began in 1920 as a mass party, with 100,000 members.

The Second World War had an even more dramatic effect, uniting the British and dividing the French. In Britain a consensus for left-wing reform developed, whereas the French experience of collaboration gave the working class a deep suspicion of the social élite — and a commitment to a Communist party that played a leading role in the Resistance.

Asked an open-ended question about whether rich people "deserved" to be so, several of Gallie's French workers referred to the war. "You need to see the past history of these people," said one. "Money doesn't fall from the sky. I knew poor people who were involved in the black market during the war and became rich. They took advantage of other people's misfortune" (p. 48). This response is related — through class consciousness — to the commonest theme: "Where you find really big fortunes, it can only have been on the back of the worker — by exploiting the worker" (p. 47).

British workers felt less strongly, only a slight majority thinking the rich didn't deserve to be so (the French thought this by a two-to-one majority), and being twice as likely to mention inheritance as a reason. "A lot of people have inherited it. You can be a complete vegetable and still be a millionaire" (p. 45). "It's been handed down.

A man did a favour for a king years ago and got land in return. They didn't earn their wealth" (p. 46).

British workers who felt the rich didn't deserve to be rich were much less likely than the French to mention exploitation or fraud as a reason. This lack of any personal wickedness on the part of the rich makes inequality more acceptable in Britain. "It's their parents and before them who amassed the riches and they don't have anything to do but spend it, but it doesn't bother me much" (p. 46). Indifference was still the main feeling towards the rich in 1985, when a Gallup poll (of the whole population, not just manual workers) found 46 per cent who were indifferent to rich people, 39 per cent who respected, admired or liked them, and only 29 per cent who envied, were irritated by or disliked them.[3] Even if it is felt to be wrong, the legal inheritance of wealth first accumulated a long time ago makes confiscating it seem less possible. "Businesses started out years ago and sons can inherit it who are stupid — in any case they haven't worked for it. There has always been money in some families. There is nothing much you can do about it." Gallie comments: "Although it is compatible with a certain contempt for the rich, it reduces the possibility of attributing evil intent" (p. 46).

This remained strikingly true in 1986, when a Gallup poll found that 55 per cent of the whole population thought the rich were "entitled to be rich", and 56 per cent that they should be "allowed to do as they pleased with their money". Although 70 per cent thought the gap between rich and poor was "too big", they saw no especial injustice in this. Only half as many thought it "unjust" that some people were much richer than others.[4] Locating the acquisition of wealth in the past — and particularly in a past that doesn't contain a recent national betrayal — also allows for uncertainty as to the morality of it. Property could be theft: "The land was stolen in the first place. They haven't earned it — they haven't worked for it." Or it could have been earned: "A lot of people are born into money. They haven't had to work for it and they don't deserve it. But I'd let them keep it as their parents worked for it and sacrificed for the sake of their heirs" (p. 46).

Lastly, Gallie suggests, the structure of post-war politics played a role. The French Left was almost always in opposition, while the British Labour Party's years in government probably both satisfied some of the working class's radical aspirations and disillusioned its hopes of achieving others. The French proportional representation voting system (1946 – 58), and later its two-ballot system, also encouraged radical party positions. The Communists could not afford to be outflanked on the left by a small party claiming to be more left-wing, whereas the British electoral system encourages the Labour Party to extend its appeal across the centre to win over marginal Tory, and now Liberal/SDP Alliance, votes. This interpretation is consistent with the dramatic decline in support for the French Communist Party since President Mitterrand's election in 1981. The Eurobarometer opinion surveys also show a decline in support for the revolutionary option to a level not much higher than Britain (in early 1986, Italy and Greece had distinctively higher scores than other European Community members).

Inequality as an incentive

Under Mrs Thatcher, the focus of the official Conservative philosophy of inequality has been on the need for incentives to drive wealth creators to ever greater achievements in the cause of national revival. In practice, the arguments for incentives hardly amount to much, and the people responsible for paying high salaries tend to fall back quite quickly on "the going rate" or market comparisons to justify them. But there is one group of people who are forced by their function to develop the philosophy of incentive: the Top Salaries Review Body. Each year this committee of eight rather well-paid men (sic) struggles with words like "weight", "calibre" and "onerous responsibilities" to come up with an argument for increasing the pay of top civil servants, judges and military brass.

Headed by Lord Plowden, an industrialist who was chairperson of Midlands metal company Tube Investments, now TI, the Review Body includes Sir Harold Atcherley, whose recreations in *Who's Who* include "skiing, good food," so at least he knows about the needs of Top Salary earners; Lord Chorley of accountants Coopers and Lybrand, who knows in detail of Top Salary earners' desire to hold on to what the Review Body recommends; and Sir Robin Ibbs, a director of ICI who earns more than the top Top Salary (he gets, as far can be made out from ICI's accounts, between £170,000 and £210,000; whereas the top Top Salary, Cabinet Secretary Sir Robert Armstrong's, is £77,400).

Mrs Thatcher has made it quite plain that arguments based simply on what allegedly "comparable" people get paid in the private sector will get sent back unmarked. Hence the adoption by the Review Body of the jargon of the free market and its emphasis on "retention" problems. This was spectacularly successful in 1985, when there were substantial revolts in both Houses of Parliament over the acceptance by the government of rises of up to 46 per cent. Well, only three went up that much, but the average rise, of 15 per cent, was still a political blunder at a critical point in the long teachers' pay dispute over a rise of 5 per cent.

The vocabulary of the market is seriously flawed, however, because it doesn't just depend on being able to prove that the people required to be mandarins, judges and Service chiefs are leaving the public sector for more highly-paid jobs outside, but that this is affecting the "quality" of those remaining as public servants.

The Review Body was sufficiently cowed by the furore over its 1985 report to put in for a total rise of only 6.5 per cent in 1986, while the rate of increase for company directors was still averaging around 10 per cent. The government, also wary, whittled down this modest (in market terms) increase to a total of 4 per cent. But the Review Body's 1986 report is interesting for its highlighting of what it thought was the central paragraph of the previous year's wisdom in the confident belief that this says it all, and that once codified on paper it is only a matter for future generations of keeping pace with inflation. The objective, carefully argued and immutable basis for the salary levels recommended in the 1985 report was that they were

> *in our opinion* . . . *adequate, no more and no less*, to ensure that these important positions in the public sector are *manned* by people of *suitable calibre*, and to do *justice* to the *onerous responsibilities* which they involve (*Ninth Report on Top Salaries*, 1986, p. 3, my emphasis).

The Review Body covers nearly 2,000 jobs. At the start of 1986, 57 of them were women, manfully manning the lower rungs of the civil service and the judiciary. There are no women in the Armed Forces covered by the Review Body (Major General and above).[5]

But it is when it comes to comparing jobs *within* the enclosure marked "Top Salaries", that the Review Body's verbal tools become really incisive, effortlessly and unambiguously making distinctions between degrees of responsibility and their associated financial rewards. In 1985, the Review Body compared various Top Salary jobs in terms of "*a realistic differential*", "*too great a difference*" and existing pay (of circuit judges) being "*by no means excessive*". The Review Body had also recommended, and the government hadn't agreed, that the top civil servants in the Ministry of Defence, the Home Office and the DHSS should be "distinguished" (that is, paid more) from the heads of other departments. On what grounds? That their jobs "were *especially heavy*". Meaning their departments are bigger. "The government decided," the Review Body admits in its 1986 report, "that there was not a sufficiently strong case" for paying these three mandarins more than the others. So what did it do? As you can expect, it argued forcefully and convincingly for its case. "We remain of the view that the *further differentiation* suggested would be *justified* in terms of *job weight*". How "heavy" is a hospital cleaner's job? What kind of burden does a "shoe shine girl" bear? So far, the government has not accepted the Review Body's recommendation.

Not all rich people think money incentive schemes are a good idea. James Beattie, chairperson of the Wolverhampton department store of the same name, says:

> I have yet to hear of a management incentive scheme which, thoroughly tested over a 10-year period, has been judged a success. The greatest defect in so-called incentive schemes is the way in which they lead to the deadly "we and they" situation within a company, the management receiving all kinds of benefits not available to others, in particular the indecently high golden hand-shake awarded on failure.

However, the lesson Beattie draws isn't necessarily the right one: "Unless British industrial companies seek to copy the kind of spirit prevailing in a good military unit, and the methods by which this is achieved, the British disease will continue to kill us." (Letter to the *Financial Times*, 23 December 1985.)

The idea that entrepreneurs require incentives in order to persuade them to take risks is contradicted by an admiring study of thirteen business tycoons by *Times* journalist William Kay (*Tycoons*, 1985). He says: "With the possible exception of Gulliver [James Gulliver of Argyll foods], none considered himself a risk taker and several positively disputed that description."

There is a socialist case for incentives, argued by, among others, R.H. Tawney: "No one thinks it inequitable that, *when a reasonable provision has been made for all*, exceptional responsibilities should be compensated by exceptional rewards" (*Equality*, p. 117, my emphasis). This sweeping statement might overlook the fact that there are genuine egalitarians who strictly believe that no one should be permitted greater material reward than anyone else — a view which needs to be dealt with by argument rather than erased by omission. What we haven't examined in much detail is the concept of just rewards. Tawney sets out the purpose of exceptional rewards for exceptional responsibilities as "a recognition of the service performed and an inducement to perform it". But neither Tawney, nor Neil Kinnock, tell us anything more about a socialist incentive policy.

Perhaps it's best left to the rich themselves to explain why they should be paid as much as they are. They are strangely unforthcoming on the subject, and it seems a bit unfair to pick on Sir John Harvey-Jones, former chairperson of ICI, just because he was prepared to speak up. But why did he think he should get paid £312,991 a year?

> The future of this country depends on a more effective industrial sector. People have to believe they can get rich by taking a top industrial job. Actually, I'm paid less than the head of one of my smaller advertising agencies, and 60 per cent of it goes back to the government (*Daily Express*, 28 May 1985).

Well, not 60 per cent perhaps; more like 49 per cent,[6] and there was his income from other directorships and his £470,500 share option profit since 1984 to consider. But his argument is clear, although it presupposes that there are not enough talented people around, and that if by some mysterious non-market process "we decide" that industry and the civil service ought to have more of this scarce commodity than they presently have, then pay rates in the City (or advertising agencies) have to be matched. But why is the "going rate" in other sectors so high? Is it necessary for 7 per cent of all main board directors and managers reporting directly to the board in the City to be earning more than £100,000 a year? And why should Sir John get a pension probably well in excess of £100,000 (impossible to work out accurately from the accounts) when from 1979 to 1982 the pensions of ICI's retired workforce rose by between 2 and 5 percentage points less than the rate of inflation? The future of this country does not appear to depend on workers and middle managers believing they can rely on a decent pension when they take an industrial job.

Income, Wealth and Power
Inequality is not just a question of one person having more money

than another. It is the holding of economic power over other people that is the heart of the matter. One of the problems for egalitarians is the focus on incomes — and the belief in the "progressive" properties of income tax — when inequality of income is a symptom, not a cause, of inequalities of wealth and power.

Neil Kinnock's attack on the "free" market was only half right:

> Now we talk about the freedom to make a lot of money. The question always posed by socialists is never whether a lot of money exists, or whether a corporation or an individual has got a lot of money, it's how did they come by it, and what are they going to do with it? The possession of wealth is not in any sense offensive. What is problematic, and in many cases offensive because it is exploitative, is how people got it. Did they secure it by gross disadvantage being inflicted upon others? And are they putting it back in the form of new investment, are they regenerating the society, or are they shipping it abroad to tax havens? (*Weekend World*, London Weekend Television, 9 February 1986.)

But the possession of wealth *is* a problem for socialists. It is the possession of wealth by the same "class" of people which perpetuates inequality from one generation to another.

Professor Bill Rubinstein wrote in 1974 of "the breakdown of the *ancien régime* of wealth in terms of the withdrawal of the wealthy from their old public functions". During the course of this century, he said, the rich withdrew from national politics, business and leadership in their communities and towns.[7] On the other hand, the rich retained control of many of the levers of power that mattered, although they may have had a lower profile, and wealth and power may have been shared out among a larger minority. Entry into private education, for example, is still extremely limited (the sector accounts for 6.6 per cent of school-children), and the declining share of wealth owned by the richest 1 per cent has partly been because of the burgeoning growth in the kinds of "passive" wealth held by the rest of the richer half of the population — houses, pension rights and insurance policies. These kinds of wealth don't confer much economic power, although they do allow economic independence. Pension wealth and insurance funds are *controlled*, although not *owned*, by the same financial élite which directs much of Britain's finance sector. It's an élite which has become a little more open socially, but not much.

What is striking about the rich is not their "withdrawal" from spheres of public life and power, but their ability to maintain much of their wealth and influence throughout the Welfare Revolution — the four decades since 1940 which were dominated by a public policy consensus, not just in the UK, in favour of universal provision of basic needs and redistribution of resources from rich to poor. Many ancient aristocratic families were taken by surprise by death duties, which in the 1940s and early 1950s raised substantial revenues, and stately homes often became a drain on family resources. But many large units of inherited wealth survived, and some developed strategies for survival and growth at a very early stage (see Chapter 9).

The royal family: a greed example

Inequality is never a matter of brute physical or even purely economic power. Differences of material well-being are enabled by cultural and social values — in Britain by a status system headed by the royal family. The *New Statesman*'s Jubilee editorial (11 February 1977) wrote that:

> The Queen is simply a very rich woman, safeguarding her wealth with all the sharpness, all the lack of sentiment or tender conscience, and all the assured complacency which have become natural to the first family of the world's most experienced capitalist class.

It was inaccurate then, and it is even more wrong now. If the Queen were actually as rich as common myth supposes, her personal wealth might be an issue. But her real role as head of the "first family" is symbolic, and the success of that symbolism was illustrated by the storm of protest the editorial and later "Anti-Jubilee" issue provoked. At the head of an angry mob of readers, Elizabeth Graham-Yooll wrote on behalf of the defenceless royals, "who have not got the privilege of reply, nor the freedoms we enjoy in our humbler state. Wealth is only relative. It is not important" (*New Statesman* Letters, 10 June 1977).

One function of the royal family is to defuse envy and anger at inequality, and it's no coincidence that the royal soap opera has really taken off since 1979. The apparent cause of the royal success story was Princess Diana and the royal wedding in 1981. But the resonance of the royal circus lies in the wider political context. The crisis of nationalism which lies behind Mrs Thatcher's appeal, the recession of 1980 and the Falklands war of 1982 all contributed to a need for a glittering escapist story.

The royal family's function of legitimising hierarchy and inequality is performed through television and the tabloid press, which is now merely an adjunct to a series of television soap operas. It's a dangerous but vital role in the cultural underpinning of the revival of the rich; dangerous because the juxtaposition of poverty and royal opulence could undermine acceptance of inequality, but vital because the only way to make such a juxtaposition palatable is to endow the opulence with the sacredness of monarchy, the unreality of soap opera and the emotion of national unity.

In the months before the marriage of Prince Andrew and Sarah Ferguson the domination of television news by commercials for "The Firm" — as the Duke of Edinburgh is reported to refer to the family — reached levels probably exceeding those of 1981. I don't know of any statistical analysis, but crude samples showed that for at least a month and a half before the wedding a "royal item" was compulsory in every mainstream news bulletin, on BBC or ITV.

This inevitably produced some awkward juxtapositions which pointed up the royal family's function. On the BBC's *Nine O'Clock News* on 25 June 1986 (almost exactly a month before Fergie's big day), the third news item was the claim that "poverty in Britain has increased by 50 per cent since the government came to power". This was a report of the Child Poverty Action Group and Low Pay Unit's estimate that the numbers of people living on or below the level of Supplementary Benefit had increased from 6 million in 1979 to 9.3 million in 1986. The report featured a single mother with three young children who lived on £59.10 a week after rent.

Next came Julia Somerville's beaming visage: "The people of Belfast had a surprise today — Prince Andrew and Sarah Ferguson dropped in for a 24-hour visit." The sycophantic voice-over purred ". . . the delight of the crowd . . . a vintage open tourer . . . a sports day for policemen [sic] and their families . . . but security must envelop royalty in Northern Ireland, even at the garden party." Cut from armed police with dogs to woman with parasol and crowd of nobs in hats on the lawn. Subtext: rich people are part and parcel of national unity and must be protected by men with guns and dogs. But interpretation is superfluous, as the voice-over continues ". . . a brave visit to Northern Ireland at a time of unease and tension. It was the sort of morale booster for ordinary citizens that earns enthusiastic applause [sound of polite clapping at garden party] across any community divide."

Then there's some real news about Israel, and to wind up . . . the treatment of the enterprising tour operator selling day coach trips of "Fergie-land" pokes gentle fun at these soft-headed provincials standing outside the snack bar *where Fergie used to get her lunch* drinking their takeaway teas in polystyrene cups, just like Fergie used to. But the purpose is straightforward: to show the devotional respect in which good citizens hold the royal family, or anyone connected with them.

According to some right-wing commentators, the financial bargain between the monarchy and the state operates in the state's favour, trading the Civil List and the royal tax exemption for "the real if unmeasurable benefit to the nation of the stabilising and unifying influence caused by the very existence of the monarchy" ("The business of monarchy", *Economist*, 21 December 1968). It is not an arrangement which the Labour Party has felt able to repudiate. Indeed, the royal salaries — the Civil List — are negotiated at the start of every reign, but were first index-linked by the Labour government in 1975. These days even veteran anti-monarchist MP Willie Hamilton is rarely heard.

But it is not the amount of the Queen's private wealth that matters. In fact, she is much less rich than the popular media likes to imply. Excluding the art collections and the Duchies of Cornwall and Lancaster themselves (they are "official" property that go with the job), the upper limit to the value of the genuinely private royal fortune was £146 million in 1986. There is absolutely no evidence to support media speculation of £1,500 million (American *People Weekly*, 1986) or £4,000 million (London Weekend Television's *Fortune* programme, August 1986). [8]

Now that the mystical unreality of the royal family is so firmly established, there's no political mileage to be gained from attacking the Queen's exemption from tax. How can you tax fictional characters? But while the royal tax-free wealth is not greatly significant of itself, it provides the model for Tory tax policy. By custom, serious tax avoidance in Britain begins with the Head of State, and a millionaire-owned press incites approval.

---

1. Jeremy Bentham, Chapter 12, "Principles of the Civil Code", *Works*, 1843, volume 1, quoted by R.H. Tawney, *Equality* (1931), George Allen and Unwin, fourth edition, 1952, p. 102.

2. Forced to choose a class, however, a majority of all Britons — let alone

manual workers — describe themselves as working-class: the 1985 British Social Attitudes Survey found 47 per cent described themselves as working-class, but it also offered the intermediate label "upper-working-class", which a further 19 per cent opted for; 26 per cent described themselves as middle-class, 2 per cent upper-middle, 4 per cent simply "poor" and 2 per cent didn't know.

3. *The Gallup Survey of Britain*, Gordon Heald and Robert Wybrow, Croom Helm 1986.

4. Gallup poll carried out in February 1986 for LWT's *Fortune* programme (August 1986).

5. Parliamentary Answer, 12 May 1986, *Hansard*, column 310.

6. Total tax bill as a proportion of salary for a married man assuming full mortgage relief and £40,000 invested in a Business Expansion Scheme, but no pension contribution relief as ICI appears to pay pensions direct to former directors (payments totalled £3.8 million in 1985). Pension relief would reduce his average tax bill to around 40 per cent: see Tricks with Tax, p. 161.

7. W.D. Rubinstein, "Men of property: occupation, inheritance and power" in *Elites and Power in British Society*, edited by Philip Stanworth and Anthony Giddens (see Bibliography, p. 187). In 1905, those who left more than £100,000 when they died were chairpersons or principal directors of 11 of the 15 largest industrial companies. Rubinstein commented that the leaders of the 15 largest companies in 1974 are unlikely to be worth the equivalent when they die. But the resurgence of business wealth through the rise in company profits and the growth of new companies and share options makes it seem more likely in the late 1980s.

8. Serious estimates of the value of the Queen's private wealth ranged up to £50 million in the early 1970s. In 1971 the Lord Chamberlain, Lord Cobbold, was sent to the Select Committee to tell MPs: "Her Majesty has been much concerned by the astronomical figures which have been bandied about in some quarters suggesting that the value of these funds may now run into £50 to £100 million or more. She wishes me to assure the committee that these suggestions are wildly exaggerated." This wasn't good enough for radical firebrands on the committee like Roy Jenkins — then deputy leader of the Labour Party — who wondered politely if Lord Cobbold could elaborate. "It can, of course, be argued from one point of view," said the future leader of the SDP, "that anyone's private fortune is their own business, though I think there are certain rather special considerations in relation to the Sovereign." This forced Lord Cobbold to return to committee to provide the following "footnotes": "First, the phrase 'wildly exaggerated' was used advisedly after full consideration. Secondly, in using the phrase 'wildly exaggerated' Her Majesty had specifically in mind the rumoured figure of £50 million and not only the even more astronomical figure suggested in some quarters." This didn't add very much, as even Roy

Jenkins noted ("Lord Cobbold will not expect me to say that achieves precision . . . but I would not wish myself to press it further"), but it does provide an upper limit to guesswork.

Leaving aside the problem of valuing the royal art collection, the stamps and so on, if we assume she had private wealth of £50 million in 1971, and saved a quarter of her income from the Duchy of Lancaster since, and update it by the yield on government securities, we arrive at the figure of £146 million in 1986, which must be an absolute ceiling. (The Duchy of Cornwall, on the income of which Prince Charles voluntarily pays 25 per cent in lieu of income tax, brought in just over £1 million in 1984 from its properties in Kennington, south London, and the West Country. Prince Charles decided to reduce his tax rate from 50 per cent on marriage in 1981, thus giving himself the biggest Married Man's Allowance in the country. Common married men get £1,320 more than the single personal allowance; he gives himself £250,000.)

The Queen may not even be the richest woman in Britain. Olga Polizzi, Trusthouse Forte's 38-year-old design director, has a shareholding in the company worth up to £50 million, and her dividends alone were £1,868,437 in 1985. She's not wealthy on account of her husband, although he was an Italian aristocrat, but because she's the eldest of Lord Forte's five daughters, and sister of Rocco, to whom Forte Senior is handing over the business. The Forte family fortune is worth considerably more than the private royal wealth, and there are several families who are richer than the Fortes: including the Grosvenors (Dukes of Westminster), the Vesteys and the Sainsburys, who are all probably worth over £1,000 million.

7. HOW RICH IS RICH?

"I call the rich those who earn £20,000 a year. It's
a different world they live in" — Roy Hattersley,
deputy leader of the Labour Party, *Tribune*,
10 May 1985.

What sort of redistribution should we be looking for in the 1980s?
Who is "too rich" and who "too poor"? The rich could be defined
simply as those who are potentially idle, who own enough capital to
be able to live off the income, but that would raise various problems,
such as the exclusion of those on very high incomes but with no
wealth.

Roy Hattersley's instinctive definition has a certain immediate
plausibility. And as for its being "a different world", he should
know, as he lives there, on his combined income as MP and
journalist. But how did the deputy leader of the Labour Party arrive
at the figure of £20,000? In any case it suffered fairly drastic inflation,
because less than a year later it had gone up by 25 per cent. On the
Jimmy Young radio programme after the 1986 Budget, "JY" said:
"Can I just ask you: when you say rich, Roy, you mean who's rich?
I mean what income are you talking about?" Knowing that what he
said would be taken down and used in evidence (it was), Roy replied:
"It's people earning more than £25,000 a year. I don't think we
should begrudge people their very high earnings; we just ought to
face the fact that if you don't tax them properly, there are penalties."
Only months later, in July 1986, it had gone up again to £27,000.
Neil Kinnock, a little more wisely, chooses to define the rich as the
top "4 or 5 per cent" in his television interviews. Other people's
definitions of the rich range from those who can afford two cars, to
millionaires.

Income and wealth distributions are always gradual curves, and in
a sense there aren't "rich" and "poor" classes, but a degree of
concentration of wealth, which is either too great or not, depending
on your politics and your position in the distribution. An aim of
conservative politics is to increase the numbers of those who feel
they have an interest in maintaining the existing degree of wealth
concentration — even if they feel that the extent of overall inequality
is morally wrong.

So if we can't define a rich person by observation, can we define the rich by reference to what people feel is "fair"?

A democratic definition of the rich

In making judgements about the rich, we are making a judgement about the degree of inequality in a society, so "rich" must be a relative term. We can compare the distribution of income or wealth in Britain with the past and with other countries, but is it possible to make judgements about a particular distribution of resources on the basis of morality? How much inequality is acceptable?

The origin of egalitarianism is the observation that many people live restricted and miserable lives which they need not do if society were ordered differently. Much left-wing analysis of society has concentrated on the nature of this restriction and misery and hence on the poor. We know, if we want to, how the freedom of a minority of the people to travel, to stay warm, to eat what they like, to entertain friends and to buy trivial things is restricted.

Any study of deprivation ought to lead straight to the triple-locked doors of the rich. It's the fact that there are "rich" people living in the same society as the deprived that gives rise to the conviction that their deprivation is needless, and that informs the hope for a better world. For socialists, the term "rich" is pejorative; for conservatives, it's merely descriptive. And the Right has an interest in restricting the description of the poor and the rich. The modern Tory obsession with "targeting" benefits is in a long tradition of trying to distinguish between the deserving and the undeserving poor. By limiting the definition of "genuine" poverty, conservatives can present extreme poverty as the only poverty. Similarly, by presenting the really rich as the only rich, conservatives can say it's not worth getting worked up about their wealth — if it were spread more equally, it would be spread exceedingly thin.

This argument has to be tackled by calculating how much money is needed to eliminate what a majority of people think of as poverty, and defining the rich as those who'd have to pay up if we started with the richest and worked down until this amount was extracted. I define "rich" as "that level of wealth which is generally regarded as unacceptable for any given level of deprivation in a society". Most people — even though they may feel that a certain level of wealth is unacceptable — wouldn't know where to draw the line, because they have no personal experience of high incomes or large amounts of capital, whereas they tend to have quite precise views about what is "unacceptably poor". But because the feeling that some people are "too rich" is directly related to moral outrage on behalf of those who are "too poor", we have to start by defining poverty.

At first sight this seems no easier than defining "the rich". But a lot of work has been done in this field. Professor Tony Atkinson, for example, has pointed out what is *not* a good "poverty line":

> While the Supplementary Benefit scale has been approved by the British Parliament as a minimum income level, it does not necessarily enjoy widespread social approval as a national minimum and may well not provide the resources required to participate in the customary activities of the society in which people live. An important objection to the use of official poverty standards is that they are based purely on money income and ignore other aspects of deprivation (*The Economics of Inequality*, p. 229).

Professor Peter Townsend has spent much of his academic career trying to define his concept of relative poverty in terms of material and cultural deprivation. Almost single-handed he opened the country's eyes in the "never had it so good" era of the late 1950s and early 1960s to the fact that a minority of the population were effectively excluded from meaningful participation in society, even though "absolute poverty" had been abolished by the creation of the welfare state. But his attempt to provide an "objective" definition of poverty based on his monumental survey of 1968 – 69 (*Poverty in the United Kingdom*) failed in the end to get away from value judgements. He found that there was an income level below which the tendency to "go without" a range of items and activities sharply increased, which he called the "poverty line". But various critics have pointed out that there's still no objective reason for taking a particular level just because life suddenly gets worse below that level. The Duke of Westminster may find, for instance, that the quality of his life becomes disproportionately worse if his wealth falls below £1,000 million.

The search for objectivity is in fact the search for a definition of poverty that everyone can agree on. Rightwingers like Sir Keith Joseph are always going to argue, as he has, that "a family is poor if it cannot afford to eat" (*Equality*). A concept of poverty is bound to be subjective because it involves a value judgement about whether it's morally right for society to allow people to subsist below a certain level — which Keith Joseph would draw rather lower than Peter Townsend.

The most convincing argument I've come across is for the "democratic" definition of poverty devised by Joanna Mack and Stewart Lansley for the television programme *Breadline Britain* in 1983. If you can't get everyone to agree on what poverty is, you can find a level below which a *majority* agree that people should not be allowed to fall.

They call poverty the "enforced lack of socially perceived necessities", by which they mean not being able to afford the things that *most people* regard as necessities, and they commissioned a MORI opinion poll to find out what they are. This cuts out all the arguments which had previously bedevilled poverty studies about what is and is not a "necessity". MORI asked people which of a list of things they felt everybody "should have in Britain today; items which you think are necessary, and which all adults should be able to afford and which they should not have to do without".

The survey produced a list of twenty-six "necessities" — things which over half of those interviewed described as necessary (in descending order of support):

> heating, indoor loo, freedom from damp, bath, a bed each, enough money for public transport, warm waterproof coat, three meals a day for children, not having to share a home, two pairs of all-weather shoes, bedroom each for different-sex children over 10, refrigerator, toys for children, carpets, celebrations for special occasions, roast joint or equivalent once a week, washing machine, new clothes, hobby or leisure activity, two hot meals a day for adults, meat/fish every other day, presents for friends or family once a year, holiday, bicycle or sports equipment for children, garden, television.

Opinions ranged from 97 per cent thinking heating a necessity to 51 per cent a television. Some of the things that got left out were a telephone (43 per cent), an outing for children once a week (40 per cent) and a night out for adults once a fortnight (36 per cent).[1]

Mack and Lansley calculated that 5 million adults and 2.5 million children in Great Britain in 1983 lacked three or more necessities. They chose the lack of three necessities (excluding those which people said they didn't want) as their starting point because it was below this point that the lack of necessities appeared to be overwhelmingly "enforced" rather than voluntary. They then refined this estimate to exclude the 10 per cent of people who lacked three or more necessities but appeared to be able to afford them.

The other adjustments they made are more controversial. They revised the figure upwards to take account of "low expectations" — the fact that many people, especially the elderly, who said they didn't want things couldn't have afforded them anyway. The size of the adjustment they make, adding 1.9 million adults, is rather arbitrary (they assume that anyone in the poorest 40 per cent of households who can't afford a necessity is suffering an "enforced lack"), but the principle is quite valid in terms of the definition of poverty they set out with. The *Breadline Britain* survey asked what people "should be *able* to afford".

They then reduced their estimate to deduct the effects of smoking; that is, making an allowance for those who would "appear to have enough money to afford the necessities if they did not smoke". But they said they didn't agree with this adjustment, and argued that "in the main it is deprivation that leads to smoking rather than the reverse" (in their book of the series, *Poor Britain*, p. 177). It may seem strange that something so apparently trivial should influence the definition of poverty, but that it does in itself favours Mack and Lansley's argument: if smoking looms so large in poor people's spending, then it's hard to dismiss it as frivolous. However, much as I share Mack and Lansley's distaste for anti-poor prejudice (sermonising about the ability of the poor to afford cigarettes is akin to "all these people on the dole have colour televisions and videos"), their argument is contradicted by the findings of their own survey. Only 14 per cent thought a packet of cigarettes every other day was a necessity, and Mack and Lansley's argument that spending on smoking should be treated as "involuntary" is precisely the sort of value judgement their approach was an attempt to get away from.

Their approach produces a minimum estimate, making a proportional adjustment to include Northern Ireland, for the number of adults in poverty in the UK in 1983 of 5.6 million.

Mack and Lansley also made a higher estimate to include people who only lacked one or two necessities, but who appeared to lack them because they couldn't afford them (because they "seriously" affected their lives). The premise of the *Breadline Britain* survey was that people ought to be recognised as poor even if they only have to go without one necessity, although in practice it's less certain that they have no choice and that Mack and Lansley have made an accurate adjustment. After making further reductions for those, including smokers, who appear able to afford the necessities they lack, this produces what I call *Breadline Britain*'s "main estimate" of 7.9 million adults in poverty. I shall refer to 5.6 million as the "lower estimate", and use it to show what effect a different definition of poverty makes.[2]

To update the *Breadline Britain* findings to 1986, I have used the official DHSS estimate of the number of families with incomes at or below the Supplementary Benefit level in 1983, and the House of Commons library's estimate of the increase in the number of families on Supplementary Benefit between 1983 and 1986 (see p. 35–6). Applying the same percentage increase, the *Breadline Britain* definition of poverty covers at least 10 million adults in 1986. (If we update the lower estimate, which excludes those lacking one or two necessities, we arrive at a figure of over 7 million.)[3]

We then need to know the amount of money that would be required to eliminate poverty. Mack and Lansley estimate that raising the income of the poor to one and a half times the Supplementary Benefit level would enable most of the poor to afford the necessities they lack — to enable everyone to live at what *most people* think is a decent standard. I've calculated (see Appendix, p. 176) that to lift 10 million adults out of poverty in April 1987 prices would cost about £12,000 million a year.

So, to how many rich people do we have to bring the benefits of socialism in order to extract — every year — the necessary sum? The method is to line them up in order of income, including notional income from their wealth, and declare a maximum: those with an income above this level have to hand over their excess. In order to raise £12,000 million in 1987, the maximum would have had to be set at an income of £22,000 a year, which would typically be made up of earned income of £16,400 a year plus the unearned income from personal wealth of £110,000. Rich couples are those with joint income of twice as much, typically joint earnings of £32,800, and joint wealth of £220,000. The earnings figure includes pensions, but not (other) income from capital — the wealth figure, which is assumed to produce a 5 per cent real rate of return, actually includes assets typically producing only £2,000 a year.

Earnings of £16,400 and wealth of £110,000 is the typical split between earnings and wealth at the borderline between rich and non-rich. Obviously some people are very rich and have low or no earnings, while others get a very high salary and spend it all. The table below shows different ways in which the £22,000 "rich threshold" could be divided between earned income and assumed income from wealth.

Earnings (per year)	Wealth
0	£440,000
£7,000	£300,000
£12,000	£200,000
£15,400	£130,000
£16,400	£111,000
£17,000	£99,000
£18,000	£79,000
£20,000	£39,000
£22,000	0

If we use the lower *Breadline Britain* estimate of the numbers in poverty, the "rich line" moves up to income of £25,500 (say, earnings of £18,000 and wealth of £150,000) for an individual. The Appendix explains how a range of other assumptions — such as about how many of those on top incomes are also top wealth-holders — affects the "rich line".

Because the very rich are higher above the average than the poor are below it, this means far fewer people are defined as rich than poor. In contrast to the 10 million adults in poverty (24 per cent of the total), my estimate for the number of rich adults on this definition is 800,000 (2 per cent of the total).

This is a moral device, *not* a tax proposal. Transferring something like £12,000 million a year is quite feasible, but it would have to come from more than just the "unacceptably rich". Just giving a lump of extra income to social security claimants and the low paid would worsen the poverty trap. And it's not very feasible simply to set a maximum and confiscate any excess: these calculations have been done on the assumption that wealth produces income, and that this income is confiscated, not the wealth itself, whereas much of personal wealth is in the form of houses, which produce no income at all. If we simply go in for confiscating wealth, three times as much money could be raised — once — from just the 20,000 millionaires and multi-millionaires, if £1 million were declared the maximum personal wealth.[4] Which is just as impractical, but the above figures give us a measurable level, a "rich line" to mirror any "poverty line", which is implied by our sense that the gap between rich and poor is too great. It relates the concept of the rich to the overall distribution of wealth; putting a value on the feeling of a majority of people that the wealth of the rich would do more good by being applied to socially useful ends than by being spent by the wealthy on themselves.

This is not a new idea. A Professor Bowley attempted a similar exercise in 1919. His aim was not to define the rich, but to show how pointless it was to try to improve the lot of the poor by transferring resources from the rich, as the "surplus" available was so small. In *Equality*, R.H. Tawney quotes Bowley's estimate of £250 million as the most that "on the extremest of reckoning can have been spent out of home-produced income by the rich or modestly well-off on anything in the nature of luxury" in the UK in 1911, after allowing for maintenance of capital investment and taxation (p. 131). Tawney compares Bowley's dismissal of this amount as hardly enough to raise wages to the crude minimum calculated by Joseph Rowntree, with the possibility of quadrupling public spending on social services, and argues for collective provision as the most effective way of getting rid of poverty.

Defining the rich in relation to the poor reflects Rawls's theory of justice (see last chapter), which focuses on the most disadvantaged member of a group. As long as there's one person who is unacceptably poor, there will be another who is unacceptably rich. It's also a "moving goalpost" definition, in that if the poor are made better-off, yet common consensus redefines poverty at higher level, then further resources should continue to be redistributed away from the rich. Conservatives are perhaps better at understanding this logic behind a socialist approach to taxation than socialists themselves. Recently, the Conservative Party has made a lot of propaganda out of the supposedly "bottomless pit" of Labour's spending commitments — allegedly £28,000 million and mostly on broadly equalising projects. The Conservative argument implies that because socially-defined poverty can never be eliminated it is unnatural, against the free market and therefore authoritarian to try. The response should be that the existence of socially-defined poverty is evidence of a democratic will to change — that we ought to strive towards equality as long as a majority of people feel that the existing level of poverty is unacceptable.

A further objection to the concept of relative poverty — and hence relative unacceptable wealth — is the scale of poverty in the Third World. Why restrict the comparative horizon to one relatively prosperous nation-state? Surely in relation to the world's poor virtually the whole British people are "unacceptably rich"? In relation to the world's poor, we are; and the alleviation of poverty in other countries should be one of the objects of enlightened public policy in the First World (the "Three Nations" analysis is replicated on a world scale).

However, practical considerations assert themselves. The primary mechanism for enabling greater equality is the state — international agencies such as multinational corporations and the United Nations have as yet little conscious power to redistribute resources, and there are also limits to the redistributive powers of local and regional agencies within countries. The definition of relative poverty is also a cultural construct, which varies in different countries, and which partly depends on rich and poor feeling themselves to be part of the same (national) community. Once the intensity with which national inequality is felt subsides, progressive countries might, like Sweden, turn national policy more purposefully towards the problem of the world North-South divide.

There are, of course, all sorts of problems with any definition of the rich, as Roy Hattersley has discovered. So far I have defined "rich" in terms of income, converting wealth into income terms (assuming that £5,000 a year is the same as a lump sum of £100,000, disregarding inflation), because it's easier to define in income terms the amount of money needed to pull the poor out of poverty. No premium has been placed on the advantages of holding wealth, although one of the most imprisoning things about poverty is the lack of any "wealth" to fall back on. "I've got £1 in the building society," Mr McGirr told the *Guardian* in a feature about the unemployed in July 1986. "That's my safety net."

The definition of the potentially idle rich is beset by the same problems. It too relies on looking at wealth in terms of the income it produces. Take, for example, two otherwise average people who win the £250,000 premium bond prize, and who thereby qualify as "rich" according to the table on p. 100, average earnings being £8,612 (median, April 1986, full-time employees). One of them could say "it won't change my life" and put it in an ethical unit trust until the day she dies, when it's bequeathed to War on Want. The other could buy a bigger house, a car, indulge his passion for chocolate and invest the rest in friends' businesses.

How do you compare the two? He gets "poorer" by the day as he dissipates his wealth, and yet is living a life of luxury; she gets "richer" as her untouched wealth increases, and yet is living a life of only average comfort.

Suppose, further, that six months later his friends' company went bust and he lost his investment. Suppose he were like a Mr A.C. Barber, who won the £250,000 premium bond prize on 3 August 1984 and three weeks later invested £100,000 in a television services company run by his friends, which went into receivership in February 1985 (we know because he sued the company to get some of the money back, and the case was reported in the *Financial Times*; court cases are one of the few ways of discovering what rich people actually do with their money).[5]

If this hypothetical male premium-bond winner spent all the rest of his prize money, he was treating it as income of £150,000 for six months — in a sense he was temporarily the equivalent of someone with an income of £300,000 a year — and hence, temporarily, well above the hypothetical female premium-bond winner in the rich league. But by now, assuming he's still on average earnings and with no wealth, he doesn't count as rich, and she still does.

In the language of economics, wealth is a measure of stocks and income a measure of flows. Stocks are measured at a point in time, while flows are measured over a period, such as a week, month or year. Our definition of the rich has so far taken no account of the passage of time: people's ages, their pension rights, lifestyle, expectations. Old people tend to be richer than young people because they've had more time to save, whereas middle-aged people often have children to pay for and a different lifestyle to maintain. Simply comparing "adults", or "households", as in Chapters 3 and 4, means comparing people at different stages of their lives in different family situations.

These problems were considered by the Royal Commission on the Distribution of Income and Wealth in 1977:

> It is possible to conceive of a notion of total wealth, encompassing all future income flows, including earnings and transfers as well as income deriving from the ownership of marketable assets. Measurement on this basis would provide in effect an estimate of potential lifetime command over resources. [But] the measurement of total wealth is no more than a theoretical possibility (*Report No 5*, p. 10).

The Commission decided that it would be better to recognise the different characteristics of the two kinds of command over resources by "presenting information on income and wealth separately but in such a way that cross-classifications can be made" (p.11). But unfortunately it didn't pursue this line of investigation before it was abolished in 1979.

Constructing a measure of "lifetime wealth" would quickly founder — even if the problems of valuing and comparing different life experiences over time could be solved — on the question of the family. How do you measure and compare the wealth of individuals, adults, adults plus dependants, nuclear families, dynasties? All of these can be measured on a "snapshot" — or wealth — basis at a point in time, but measuring the lifetime wealth of an individual would involve accounting for shared use of resources at different times.

Private education in particular is a sophist's speciality: is it a family or an individual benefit? Should the cost of private education be regarded as the income of the child or is it an asset to be counted as part of parental wealth? Although the parent receives no direct benefit as an individual, money spent on private education could have been spent on other items that could have been counted as individual wealth. We could take a "market" view and say that because the parent chooses to spend the money on private education, then it's as much an item of personal consumption as a fridge-freezer. But how do you value the purchase of privilege? Not only is the privilege an asset for little Edward, who is more likely to be able to get a job as something in the City, but his parents can sleep easier at night and could be regarded as possessing an intangible asset.

Relative riches
The idea that unacceptable poverty or wealth are subjective judgements that change over time is one that catches out one government after another. Whenever you hear a government claim that pensioners or claimants, or even the NHS, are getting "more in real terms than ever before", you ought to be on your guard, because it probably means they are getting less in terms of what society can afford and may want to afford, selfish though it supposedly is.

On the level of Supplementary Benefit, the Thatcher government is caught in the same trap that has also tripped up Labour governments: if it increases the real value of Supplementary Benefit do-gooding pressure groups will run around saying there are more people in poverty. The only trouble is that they are usually right. If you increase the real value of Supplementary Benefit by a "tiny weeny bit" at a time when average earnings are racing ahead of prices by 5 per cent a year, and top earnings by even more, the poor may be better off in *absolute* terms, but still be poorer *relative to* the rest of society.

The question of what to do after the creation of the welfare state had apparently abolished absolute poverty in Britain first became a live issue with the rediscovery of poverty in the late 1950s. Academics Brian Abel-Smith, Peter Townsend and Richard Titmuss "discovered" the facts that many old people in particular were too proud to take up their entitlement to National Assistance (the precursor of Supplementary Benefit), that the numbers of people with incomes at or below the National Assistance level was increasing, and that the poor included a substantial number of children. In terms that sound depressingly familiar today, Townsend's analyses of Labour Ministry figures in 1962 and 1963 showed that the numbers of people living at or below the National Assistance level had almost doubled, from 4 million in 1953 to 7.5 million in 1960.

This small group of academics was quickly disillusioned by the election of the Wilson government in 1964, and formed the Child Poverty Action Group in 1965 to press the case for child benefits. But, according to Michael McCarthy in his history of CPAG, "by the summer of 1968 it was apparent that CPAG's influence upon the Labour government had not been as great as the executive committee had hoped for" (*Campaigning for the Poor*, p. 104). After initially raising old age pensions and social security benefits, the government appointed the Houghton inquiry into the benefits system to delay further measures and social security slipped down the list of priorities. Prescription charges had been brought back in, and the Wilson government had started making cuts in social security spending. CPAG underwent a radical change in direction with the appointment of Frank Field as director in 1969. The group went on the offensive against the Labour government's record, most controversially launching the "Poor Get Poorer Under Labour" campaign in the run-up to the 1970 election.

It wasn't true that the poor had got poorer; not only had their real standard of living risen since 1964, but they had also kept up with the general increase in the nation's living standards, with a slight falling back since 1968. The argument in 1970 — which split the left-of-centre academic establishment — might seem in retrospect a luxury. But it has not yet been resolved. The campaign went to the heart of Labour's post-war philosophical problem — what next after the welfare state? Should a Labour government, having redistributed resources to meet "concrete" human needs for health care, education and the avoidance of destitution, then go on to redistribute incomes to meet the "abstract" human need for full participation in society? Or would redistribution on such a scale reduce the standard of living of too many comfortably-off "ordinary people"?

It was when it was faced with this choice — at a time of economic stagnation — that the Callaghan government lost its way. The choice was resolved by the election of a Conservative government which, for example, ended the link between pensions and average earnings, which had been designed to ensure for pensioners the same *relative* share of national income. If it had been maintained, basic pensions would now be 7 or 8 per cent higher (£4.55 a week more for couples), which is a measure of the increasing *relative* poverty of pensioners who don't have a pension from their job or significant amounts of wealth — which is about 3 million of the 9 million total.

As real earnings for those in work rise, the majority definition of the poverty level by the *Breadline Britain* method will also rise, as people decide that some of the items now considered luxuries are essential after all.

---

1. The *Breadline Britain* survey was carried out for London Weekend Television by Market and Opinion Research International (MORI) between 15 and 24 February 1983 interviewing 1,174 people at 80 places in Great Britain. The figure for a television being a necessity is subject to sampling error (plus or minus 3 per cent at 95 per cent tolerance). Thirty-five items were listed, of which 26 were considered necessities by over 50 per cent of the sample, with an average for all items of 64 per cent. There are problems with this kind of survey. The 35 items were chosen arbitrarily, and we don't know how their estimates for the numbers in poverty would change if other "necessities" could be identified. There are also logical problems with the form of the questions. For example, the "least necessary" item — a packet of cigarettes every other day, which only 14 per cent thought a "necessity" — is relatively cheap, and hence something it's logically difficult to say people should not be "*able* to afford". Further, it's possible that people don't give truthful or particularly durable answers to this kind of question, and describe some things as "necessities" simply because they don't want to appear mean to the interviewer.

2. Mack and Lansley (*Poor Britain*, George Allen and Unwin 1985) describe the range of their estimates as between 6 and 12 million, which includes children. I have ignored another possible refinement offered by the authors, to take account only of the enforced lack of those necessities which are

"overwhelmingly" regarded as such by those interviewed by MORI. This again defeats the aim of objectivity by rejecting the opinion of a simple majority.

3. DHSS figure for number of people in families receiving Supplementary Benefit or on incomes below Supplementary Benefit level, Great Britain 1983: 8.910 million ("Low Income Families 1983", July 1986), grossed up to UK in proportion to population: 9.170 million. Commons library estimate of Supplementary Benefit recipients and dependants, UK, 6 May 1986: 9.053 million (commissioned by Frank Field, unpublished July 1986); plus DHSS estimate for numbers not receiving Supplementary Benefit but on incomes below Supplementary Benefit level, Great Britain 1983, 2.780 million, grossed up for UK 2.861 million (1986 minimum); total UK 1986: 11.914 million. Increase of 30 per cent applied to *Breadline Britain* main 1983 figure (7.9 million) is 10.26 million; "low" 1983 figure (5.6 million) is 7.28 million.

4. Derived from Professor Anthony Shorrocks's forward projection to 1986 from the Inland Revenue's 1983 estimate of the distribution of personal wealth excluding pension rights. He estimated that there were 20,000 individuals worth more than £1 million, who owned 4.2 per cent of total personal wealth (*New Society*, 22 August 1986) which was about £1,000,000 million — an average of at least £2 million each. The "surplus" over £1 million each is therefore at least £20,000 million.

5. He didn't succeed. *Financial Times*, 18 July 1986.

8. MERGING INTO THE SCENERY

"If we are still here it is because you want us. If you
did not we would have been got rid of." — Duke of
Westminster, *Sunday Times*, 8 October 1978.

The previous chapter came up with a working definition of those
who are "too rich" by democratic egalitarian standards. But from
there to redistribution is a very difficult journey. One of the most
important factors in any future effort at redistribution is the
existence of a popular will to tackle inequality. But the evidence is
that most people, although they have negative views about the rich,
do not support attempts to divest them of their wealth. Why?

The rich themselves are generally very careful not to present themselves too publicly as excessively fortunate. They alternately regard
their position as accidental and deserved, a burden or a blessing, and
always bearing a heavy responsibility both to their heirs and the
"less fortunate".

"Not many children are . . . cursed, blessed — I'm not quite sure
what's the right word — with a sixty-room house," says the mother
of Alexander, a *Citizen 2000* (Channel Four's television programme
about children who will be eighteen in the year 2000). "Though I
think having a nanny's an essential, it never occurs to me that I'm
privileged in any way at all."

As the aristocracy has always done, Gerald Grosvenor, the sixth
Duke of Westminster, says "I'm just the caretaker for future
generations," implying that he lives frugally (he drives a £65,000
Aston Martin Lagonda) to save his descendants from the humiliation
of having to live on Supplementary Benefit. His sister, the Duchess
of Roxburghe, is much the same. Living in Floors Castle, she is
frightened her three children will

> get a bit grand if they think life is one long castle, and they [might]
> imagine they're a bit more special because they don't live in a
> council house. Rosie [royal bridesmaid Lady Rosanagh Innes-Ker,
> aged seven] is slightly aware already, so I've told her the castle is
> not really our house but something we have to look after, and
> we're very lucky to be living here. [But] although the place is vast,
> we can't have that many people to stay — twenty-one at a squeeze
> — because there aren't enough bathrooms.

"Like many other busy mothers," wrote Douglas Keay in a *Woman's Own* royal exclusive, "the Duchess told me she suffers constant guilt about not spending enough time with her children. Besides the demands of the castle and the estate, there's also the involvement with charity." And then there are the regrets, the missed opportunities. "I'd like to have been a nurse, so that at least people would know I could do something professionally," said the Duchess (*Woman's Own*, 26 July 1986). If the Duke and Duchess earn interest at a real rate of 5 per cent a year on their £30 million fortune, they make £4,120 a day — more than a student nurse gets in a year.

Other aristocrats deny that they are rich at all. The Duke of Norfolk goes as far as to finger fellow aristocrats, the Cavendishes: "We're not like Chatsworth or any of those places. Death duties and the division of the estate have seen to that. In no way am I a rich man. People think I have footmen. Actually I clean my own shoes." The Duke of Buccleuch is similarly dismissive, angrily rejecting claims that he's Scotland's richest man: "Landowners are, in the main, only wealthy if they cease to be landowners." The most famous disclaimer was Prince Philip's "we go into the red next year" claim in 1969. By this he meant that his wife would have to dip into her burgeoning private wealth for the first time. In Jubilee Year, 1977, he told the *Sunday Mirror* that "falling living standards for many will bring us all back to a greater sense of reality". He had just had a pay rise to £85,000 a year.

It's rather harder to claim that a high salary represents an heirloom to be safeguarded for future generations, or that its maintenance costs are prohibitively steep. But one of *the* sights of the 1980s is that of highly-paid managers simply forgetting that they had had a pay rise. Colin Perry, chair of Birmingham Mint coin company and of the CBI's West Midlands region, appealed to fellow employers in April 1986 to keep pay rises below 4 per cent. In July 1986 it was revealed that he'd just taken a 30 per cent pay rise to £58,049. A company spokesperson explained that most of the rise was a profit-related bonus, and that his basic salary had only risen by 5 per cent, "in line" with the rise paid to the workforce. The numbers of the workforce were cut from 530 to 480 over the year.[1]

Every year, the CBI urges its members not to hand out "un-justified" pay rises. In September 1986, Director General Sir Terence Beckett described pay rises above those justified by productivity increases as "theft" from the community. Meanwhile the average pay rise enjoyed by the sixty-two company chairpersons and chief executives on the CBI's President's Committee was 14 per cent — twice the average for everybody else lucky enough to be in work.[2] According to the annual Charterhouse salary survey for 1985/86, a quarter of all company chairpersons had total pay increases of more than 40 per cent. This is no doubt justified by the profits their companies are making.

There are some curious ideas around about profits, and who makes them. During the Wapping dispute between the printworkers and Rupert Murdoch, employment minister Kenneth Clarke attacked "Fleet Street fat cats in the print unions" who had "priced themselves into a position where Mr Murdoch presumably judged it worthwhile to start again from scratch" (*Financial Times*, 4 March 1986). What Conservatives find so objectionable about high earnings in the — profitable — print industry is that the recipients of them are working-class. Tory ministers do not call dentists, stockbrokers or company executives "fat cats". But many of these "professionals" have priced themselves into a position where some people might judge it worthwhile to start again from scratch.

In January 1986, jobless figures refused to respond to massaging, let alone to monetarism, and Conservative backbenchers were becoming restless. In an effort to hold the ideological line, a former Tory GLC councillor called Cyril Taylor organised a conference on "employment".

It was attended by fifty carefully-chosen people with a close personal knowledge and understanding of unemployment. These included Sir Michael Edwardes, who appeared on p. 32 (£383,000 for losing his job at ICL computers in 1983 and about another £200,000 two years later at Dunlop); Jeffrey Archer ("I was unemployed with debts of £400,000. I know what unemployment is like and a lot of it is getting off your backside and finding a job"), conservatively estimated to have made £5 million from his books; Sir Ronald Halstead (£407,386 handshake for being made unemployed by Beecham in 1985), treasurer of the Tory think tank the Centre for Policy Studies; and a wide cross section of others, including those who had never been unemployed in their lives, having inherited the job, like Jonathan Gestetner of Gestetner copiers and Rocco Forte of Trusthouse Forte. Mrs Thatcher was also there, taking soundings among people who inhabit the "real world" and know about its problems.

"No speaker suggested that the high level of unemployment could be brought down by means of large government spending in order directly to subsidise the creation of jobs," writes Taylor in his summary, published later as a pamphlet by the Centre for Policy Studies (*Employment Examined: the Right approach to more jobs*). Nor did any speaker suggest that the level of their remuneration could be brought down by means of large transfers to unemployed construction workers to build hospitals. So what did they suggest we try instead?

- Unemployment benefit should be cut from twelve months to six,
- planning controls should be relaxed, and
- rent controls should be phased out.

That should do the trick. In fact, the conference produced rapid results. The important thing is to put job seekers in touch with potential employers. Six months later Jonathan Gestetner announced that Sir Ronald Halstead had been appointed to the board of Gestetner Holdings as a non-executive director.

But how did these "distinguished industrialists, civil servants and politicians" arrive at their conclusions? They started by debunking the notion that there was more unemployment in the North of the country, and that the South East had relatively low unemployment. True, there are some exceptions to the rule. "Given the behaviour of Liverpool's local council, its rate of 21 per cent unemployed, four times the level of Winchester, is only to be expected," says Taylor. But "whatever the overall averages for regions, the employment figures for individual towns clearly demonstrate that there is no uniform North-South divide. On the other hand, there *is* a divide between the inner cities which have been allowed to decay, *often aided by the politics they have pursued*, and the outlying suburbs and rural market towns which have determined to thrive." (My emphasis.)

The dire consequences of voting Labour are incontrovertibly proven by comparing some London boroughs, says Taylor, summarising the wisdom of the assembled experts: "You can pass from Hackney, whose unemployment is among the worst in the country, a few miles down the road to Westminster and the City of London where vacancies for many jobs are hard to fill."

The residents of these decaying areas often don't want to work. "A substantial portion of those drawing unemployment benefit, perhaps as many as half a million, might well find jobs if a financial

incentive in the form of tax reductions encouraged them to do so."
Half a million is a very round number.

"Very welcome" are government schemes to subsidise workers or
employers who take or provide low-paid jobs. (See p. 50: the taxpayer rewards employers with £15 a week if they take on new
eighteen- or nineteen-year-olds at wages of less than £55 a week
under the New Workers' Scheme, or employees who have been unemployed for a year with £20 a week if they take on work at less than
£80.) Of course this interference by the "nanny" state to depress low
pay only gives further encouragement to Labour voters to stay on
the dole, so at the same time the lush benefits provided to the unemployed must be cut back. From their personal experience, Tory
MP Ralph Howell, Sir Michael Edwardes and Professor Patrick
Minford were able to describe the life of luxury on the dole,
"drawing unemployment benefit, rates rebate, rent rebate and the
host of other allowances available". (Although they don't know that
rent and rates rebates have been replaced by housing benefit, they
are no doubt fully informed as to this cornucopia of "other
allowances".)

In support of his colleagues' unanimous recommendation that unemployment benefit be cut from twelve months to six, Taylor
quotes from William Beveridge's White Paper of 1944. And it's a
good thing he does, because the passage quoted directly contradicts
him. "Six months for adults would perhaps be a reasonable *average*
period of benefit without conditions," says Beveridge, after stressing
that this period "might be extended in times of high unemployment
and reduced in times of good employment". Luckily Employment
Secretary Lord Young was on hand to remind the conference that, if
we don't concentrate morbidly on the numbers of people out of
work, this *is* a time of "good employment".

But Beveridge hasn't finished fighting back. "Men and women in
receipt of unemployment benefit cannot be allowed to hold out
indefinitely for work of the type to which they are used or in their
present place of residence," Taylor's quotation goes on, "if there is
work which they could do available *at the standard wage* for that
work." (My emphasis.) Something under £55 a week was probably
not what the father of the welfare state had in mind.

Finally, the conference turned its collective wisdom to the
problem of people who won't move to parts of the country where
there are jobs. Cyril Taylor's colleagues, most of whom own at least
two homes, demonstrated their unerring grasp of the issue. They

avoided the easy solutions like the issue of tents and corrugated iron (on loan): in a civilised society people ought to be allowed to live in houses. Luckily this is quite simple. "The problem of lack of private rented accommodation could and should be solved speedily. The present Rent Acts should be repealed forthwith." These archaic/ socialist statutes "have reduced private rented accommodation to just 10 per cent of the total housing stock from a peak of nearly 50 per cent in 1945, and severely restrict the mobility of labour". Curiously, no one mentioned the much more important role of mortgage tax subsidy for home ownership as a cause of the shortage of rented housing. No doubt by the time this book is published the campaign to repeal the Rent Acts will have succeeded, and we shall see, on new lettings at least, the labour-mobilising effects of high rents in the South East. But will people who can't move south because they can't afford an expensive mortgage be flooding into the capital, eager to pay unregulated sky-high rents instead?

This is *the* phenomenon of the 1980s; those who are doing extremely well financially berating those who are already doing badly for not being prepared to do worse still, and coming up with entirely irrelevant proposals. Add in a touch of "I know what it's like," or even "my father knew what it was like" and you have one of the most sickening sights of the past eight years. Nevertheless, this sort of talk is still couched in "sake of the nation" terms. It is not, explicitly, an I'm-all-right-Jack argument but, interestingly, there is some evidence that this attitude is now making a comeback.

The attitudes of the four specimens hooked by "The Fishing Party", (BBC2, 28 February 1986) aren't necessarily typical. But the programme exposed the loud amoral brutality of a particular species of the pointlessly rich. Two commodity brokers, who each claimed to make half a million pounds "in a good year", and two of their friends discussed the state of the world and drank on a boat in the Pentland Firth. They'd invited the BBC to film their bid to catch a record skate and instead provided an invaluable insight into the minds of right-wing Hooray Henrys.

Hanging should be reintroduced, said Guy. "I don't know how many men have gone to the gallows that shouldn't have. Ninety per cent is good enough for me." Guy's friend Henry Carew thought the unemployed "represent a threat to security, to stability, to law and order". He added — unnecessarily — that he would like to be an MP. Guy wasn't sure that there was any need. "Many of our friends worry about the aggressive young men of the loony Left. I think the Armed Forces might be a bit concerned about the result of the next election. I don't think it would take very much for a military unit to take control of London, the country, the government."

They may have been hamming it up for the cameras, but aggression is back in fashion among the upper classes. After many decades of being coy, people like Guy Cheyney feel free to express class hatred from the top. People like him have always said things like that in private, and most of them would still think it a bit off to go public. But Auberon Waugh's *Private Eye* column acted to draw to the surface the deeply anti-democratic, racist and anti-working-class traits of the Conservative character, and these can be expounded much more freely, and without the cover of uncertain "humour", in the serious press: first the *Mail* and now the *Daily* and *Sunday Telegraph*. Indeed Peregrine Worsthorne, editor of the *Sunday Telegraph*, described the message of Thatcherism as: "Yobboes and morons either conform or go under; under her rule, the productive elements do so well that society can at least afford a large police force" (7 September 1986).

Back in 1978, Worsthorne's friend Maurice Cowling had described the basic power relations in society in a more circumspect, but perhaps more sinister way:

> The Conservative conception of a social structure not only assumes that marked inequalities are inevitable but also declines to justify them because their inevitability makes justification unnecessary. To decline justification of the principle is not to say that there cannot be discussion of the content. It is not the principle or the discussion, however, but the balance of operative power that determines the outcome, and it is difficult to see how it could be otherwise (*Conservative Essays*, p. 11).

Peregrine Worsthorne later developed the argument, in a more populist vein of mystical fatalism. In the *Sunday Telegraph* colour supplement of 19 October 1986, he wrote a short but very sharp piece of vitriol about how difficult it was to be patriotic about Britain today:

> To be frank it would not be difficult for me to become disloyal to this country. If a far-left government came to power, abolished the monarchy, nationalised private property, set up people's courts — did all the things, for example, advocated by Tony Benn — treason

would become an option very much worth considering. I can well imagine myself being a party to some CIA plot to destabilise a left-wing militant British government.

It was fairly unremarkable to students of Worsthorne's brand of faintly fascist nostalgia. What was remarkable was the chord it touched with *Sunday Telegraph* readers, 178 of whom wrote to thank their editor for, for example, "expressing my feelings so succinctly".

Cowling had described this inner core of class Conservatism eight years earlier, in much more abstract language, and had not then been taken seriously.

> The Conservative party exists now, as at any other time since 1886, because those who perform the duties or acquire the benefits connected with inequality do not want democratic arrangements to break down. They judge it better if possible to get part of what they want by acting effectively through the parliamentary system than to get a bigger proportion under some other sort of regime. They accept the fact that a balancing of costs is involved and that, if the price that is paid for parliamentary government is too high, there will be those who will want parliamentary arrangements superseded. (*Conservative Essays*, p. 11.)

Guy Cheyney is the extreme example of this, and some of his views are certainly not typical. But on a much more tasteful level, people from many walks of life are finding that it is no longer not done to talk about money.

These changing attitudes have been chronicled in the *Financial Times*. In 1968, when the paper started its feature called "How to Spend It", it was thought vulgarly amusing. In the 1970s readers wrote to complain that it was offensive. In 1986, however, it recommends outfits costing £1,120 for women wanting to keep up with the "much sharper, much more elegant" New York fashion outline.

For the new aristocracy of the Boom at the Top, "How to Spend It" now provides a valuable service. Business tycoons and the young City rich work long hours and can't take much holiday and need to know how to stop it piling up oppressively. Instant good taste is required in wine, paintings, furniture, décor, especially if they can be bought through the Business Expansion Scheme when the taxpayer chips in 60 per cent of the cost.

Nevertheless, the rich in general have a great deal to gain from minimising their separateness from the rest of the population, where possible. Their tactic is to ally themselves with the middle class, and it is a sensible one, for if you are one of the Have Lots, it is surely better to keep the Haves on your side than to let them side with the Have Nots.

If the rich try to play down how different they are, they are by no means unsuccessful. The English attitude to money, according to the *Tatler* (September 1985), is that

> if you are born with lots of money, you are taught that your life's chief purpose will be the securing of an equivalent or greater sum to be passed to your heir on your death. And if born with money and a title, you are taught to see these as quite interesting enough. Any further development of character or interests might attract attention.

One of the greatest barriers to an assault on the rich is the fact that they are not necessarily easily perceptible as a separate class. They are not obviously the owners of the factors of production; they are not leisured (although many of them could afford to be) and they do not have a distinct political affiliation.

Opinion surveys show that most people in Britain, asked to identify classes, spontaneously list three (usually upper, middle and working, sometimes aristocracy at the top and lower at the bottom, but always middle in the middle). In the terms in which class is perceived these days — property, education and occupation — the rich are simply not readily distinguishable from much of the middle class. The middle class, as a result, believes it has interests in common.

To take housing first. The difference between owner-occupation and council-renting is probably one of the strongest class indicators. The choice between owner-occupation and council tenancy is a rigid one that tends not to be reversed after the first three years of marriage ("household formation" in the sociological jargon). Once your tenure is decided, it is like the choice of school, in that it affects the rest of your life chances, and those of your children. Only 3 per cent of couples both of whose parents owned their own homes became council tenants in the late 1970s.[3] But there is one exception to this rigidity. Since 1979 the Conservatives have provided the equivalent of adult education classes at private schools, by giving older council tenants in better-paid skilled or white-collar jobs, or with savings, the chance to cross the class divide by buying their council houses.

The transformation of the pattern of housing tenure in Britain since the war reflects and effects changes in the class structure. In the forty years since the war, the proportion of homes which are owner-occupied has doubled from 30 to 60 per cent. On the other hand, the proportion of private rented homes has fallen from 50 per cent to less than 10 per cent, and that of council housing has increased but is now decreasing.

Access to owner-occupation is by income as well as wealth, while access to council tenancy is by waiting (and need). This means that owner-occupiers tend to postpone having children until they have got over the initial high costs of a mortgage, while council tenants have an incentive to have children early, because of the greater waiting-list priority. So, at the crucial stage of household formation, owner-occupied households tend to consist of two relatively high earners with no children but high housing costs, while council households tend (and this is a broad generalisation) to consist of a low paid man and a non-working wife with young children and low housing costs.[4] But the housing "costs" of owner-occupiers are in fact an investment in appreciating assets; added to their existing advantages of high pay, two incomes and postponed costs of child-rearing, is the advantage of investment in their own housing, which is also going up in value by more than inflation.

Owner-occupation, with its attendant advantages, is one of the things the middle classes have in common with the rich and indeed the super-rich. On a much smaller scale, their interest on this issue is absolutely allied with their richer counterparts. They will benefit in the same way as the very rich, although by a considerably smaller amount, from the time-bomb effect as the home owners of the first boom in owner-occupation in the 1930s steadily die and leave their accumulated and inflated investment in their homes to their already home-owning children.

The importance of this shared interest is obvious. It means that any redistributive measures that attack the advantages of property ownership are seen as an attack on the middle class as well as on the very rich, even though the latter lose considerably more. The same applies to any potential attack on the second class indicator — private education. Again, the Thatcher government has widened social divisions through its assault on the state sector, in effect hardening the divisions of a three-tier education system. The top, private tier is accessible to hard cash, and has expanded from around 6 to 6.6 per cent of children between 1979 and 1985 (in England). The second tier, of "good" comprehensives and the remaining few grammar schools, is accessible through wealth in the form of house prices in desirable catchment areas, and, shamefully, parents' contributions to the costs of books and equipment which can make a considerable difference. The third tier is the minority of underfunded comprehensives, without adequate means to finance themselves.

Just as housing is the means by which differences in wealth between the middle and poorer "classes" are magnified and to some extent transmitted over generations, so education perpetuates differences in the wealth of the middle and richer "classes". But the middle class are allied with the rich over education in two ways. First, not all fee-paying parents are very rich. Secondly, the definition of a successful state school has increasingly come to be the one which most closely resembles the education available in the private sector — uniform, lots of homework, and so on. So that even when parents don't pay for private education or can't afford to do so there is very little support for the idea that private education, the chief transmitter of inequality, should be phased out, or even have its tax privileges honed down. Just as in the field of owner-occupation, an attack on institutions which are of overwhelming benefit to the very rich is seen by the middle class as an attack on themselves.

The third class indicator of the 1980s is your job. Once again, the experience of the middle class has more in common with that of the very rich than with that of the poor. The labour situations of the three groups are different, it is true. The poor and the middle class can only obtain income by virtue of their labour — "by hand or by brain" as Sidney Webb's Labour Party constitution has it — or their citizenship (their entitlement to social security), while the potentially idle are, of course, just that. However, some of the people we define as rich are not potentially idle, in that they have high incomes but not much wealth. More importantly, the potentially idle do not, in general, make use of that privilege. They tend to work, and they tend to work in occupations that are not closed to the middle class such as law or banking.

This is most emphatically not to argue that class distinctions are non-existent and that the only different thing about the rich is that they have more money. Income and wealth divisions certainly do not correlate exactly with the division between the upper class and the next one down (take your pick: middle, upper-middle, intermediate, professional and managerial, B or non-U), but there are class structures that influence financial inequalities. It's partly through those class structures that the Conservative government has increased inequality since 1979 — by adjusting the legal and cultural framework to allow the ruling class to use its power more freely. What is true, though, is that in terms of common interests the Have Lots and the Haves are, on several crucial indicators, much closer to each other than to the Have Nots — and that it is almost impossible to target the rich in a way that does not appear also to target the less rich. Go for inheritance more rigorously and anyone with a house to pass on feels threatened; relax Capital Transfer Tax and much of the middle class feels smiled upon. The concessions, and the cultural prejudices, that make the rich rich, also benefit the middle-class non-rich. The real losers are the poor.

George M (not his real name) is a rich man. He inherited and expanded a manufacturing business, and lives in a million-pound house in Hampstead. Apart from saying "in this century my family has been dispossessed four or five times," his views are not noticeably different from any of the middle class. He's keen on private enterprise, but denies being a Conservative. "Politically I think I'm a reasonable chap. I read the *Guardian*, and I've been taking the *Independent* from the day it started." So how does he justify inheritance? "Well, I know it sounds dead corny, but I was taken into the factory when I was seven." It's a way of developing commitment. He also relates it to incentive. "If you're going to enjoy ownership, part of the enjoyment of it is being able to pass it on." Isn't that an unfair way of selecting from the next generation? "Not at all. It's a Darwinian process — it automatically results in the most able people running things." But it's a Darwinian process at the level of families: sometimes heirs are the worst people for the job. George agrees: "In some cases trustees would have to make decisions."

What would be the ideal tax system? "No one objects to paying tax out of income. The levels at which you start paying tax are far too low. But beyond that one hasn't got too much to complain about. Basically, I don't care what happens as long as one is on a par with everyone else — with France, West Germany and the rest of Europe. Of course the top rate should start at seventy or eighty grand, but you can't have everything."

I presumed he'd made arrangements to insure himself against a Labour government. . . . "Young man, you presume absolutely wrongly. All my wealth is in this country. Ninety per cent of my assets are in a manufacturing business. But that just goes to show you what a silly idea a wealth tax is: how can you tax a manufacturing business? Anyway, I have a comfortable lifestyle, which I will keep up — if tax rates go up I will simply take more out of the business. If one feels morally disapproved of . . . like the political atmosphere in Britain in the late 1970s . . . the Labour government was making people *feel* they've been squeezed, and if they hadn't been, as if they were *about* to be — and then they devoted all their energies into trying to avoid it." I asked if he had any servants. "Now look. My wife works very long hours. I have two children aged three and four. What do you think I do?" Employ a nanny and a cleaner. "Right. That's exactly what I've got. My wife is the director of a public company, and she can earn ten times as much as we pay a nanny. It doesn't make sense for her to stay at home. I've had a fiscal theory for ten years or so now — that personal employment should be tax deductible; it's common sense, it would create employment and increase tax revenue [from the underground economy]. I mean, our daily is 'unemployed' and receives a housing allowance and all sorts of things." He seemed a little defensive about having domestic help. "No, no. No. I don't feel uncomfortable at all. And I don't have a chauffeur. The idea of having a man outside waiting for me is something I don't like at all. I think most people I know feel that. I used to live opposite X [a Labour minister in the 1974–79 government], and it used to amaze me. His man always used to arrive half an hour early. I used to watch him sitting there reading his paper while X was inside finishing his toast. It was bananas."

---

1. *Daily Telegraph*, 29 July 1986.

2. Labour Research Department, *Labour Research*, November 1986. The median salary of the sixty-two was £86,736, 14 per cent of which was a cash increase of £204 a week — an increase alone worth more than the amount that two-thirds of workers earn.

3. Study by Janet Madge and Colin Brown of 900 couples in Wandsworth, Hertfordshire and Nottingham 1975–77, cited by Hamnett (see Note 4 below).

4. This analysis is supported by research, such as that cited by Chris Hamnett, "Who gets to own?", *New Society*, 25 July 1986. Bernard Ineichen at Bristol University studied 200 newly-married couples in the Bristol area and concluded that young couples had to make decisions which "create an expanding social gulf between owner-occupiers and council tenants". –

9. WHY RICH PEOPLE ARE RICH

> "All in these islands hitherto have had the
> opportunity, it may be by brains which have come
> to them by their fathers or mothers, or by example
> and upbringing coupled with application,
> industry and honesty, to achieve what is called
> success in the world. From duke's son to cook's
> son, they have all had their chance." — Lord
> Inchcape, letter to *The Times*, 28 April 1930;
> quoted by R. H. Tawney, *Equality*, p. 121.

If a reforming government is to bring about greater equality, it must know how people come to be rich in the first place. In Britain what Tawney called "the social poison of inheritance" is still the most important source of original wealth for the rich, at whatever level "rich" is defined. The importance of inheritance has declined since the 1950s, but is probably still twice as great as in the United States (where land ownership was never as concentrated as it once was in Britain).

People who don't have significant money to begin with mainly become rich in two ways: selling their own labour, or selling other people's. Those who sell themselves do it either as a star performer in pop, sport or bond dealing, usually shining briefly but piling it high, or by saving over a period of time in a high-paid but less conspicuous job, such as medicine or the law. But most of the new rich become so by selling other people's labour, through new, expanding or reorganised businesses.

In their definitive study of inheritance, Professor Harbury and Dr Hitchens found, using various definitions of rich, that, in the 1950s and 1970s, "between two-thirds and four-fifths of those who died rich owed their wealth to inheritances and the rest to entrepreneurship and luck" (*Inheritance and Wealth Inequality in Britain*, p. 131). Bill Rubinstein updated this research by tracing the wealth of millionaires who died in 1984 and 1985 for London Weekend Television's *Fortune* programme. He found that three-quarters of them had inherited over £10,000 — usually a substantial sum at the time they inherited it. His study wasn't directly comparable with that of Harbury and Hitchens, but he found that the proportion of millionaires who were entirely "self-made" had doubled from 10 to 20 per cent over the post-war period.

The original Harbury–Hitchens study found "virtually no change in the importance of fathers' wealth among top male wealth leavers" between the 1920s and the 1950s. "Between the 1950s and the 1970s, however, the proportions of rich sons having rich fathers tended to decline", although this could be explained by the rise in tax avoidance and the fall in family size over the period. They found that two-thirds of the sons of rich fathers (in two samples of those who died in 1902 and the 1920s) failed to keep up the value of their inheritance, whereas one third increased it (by more than inflation). They also found that marriage is not a particularly important source of wealth: only one in seven rich sons with poor fathers had rich fathers-in-law.

The Royal Commission on the Distribution of Income and Wealth carried out research of a different kind, based on a sample of estates left by those who died in 1973. From the amounts of money left to individuals (rather than charities and so on), the Commission estimated the total *volume* of inherited wealth in Britain at that date. On this basis, known as the "perpetual inventory method", the Commission estimated that 25 per cent of total wealth in 1973 was inherited (*Report No 5*, p. 194). This figure included an assumption for the amount of gifts made during the donor's lifetime, at constant prices, but *excluded* the return on inherited wealth earned by the inheritor.

This figure is twice as much as the estimated proportion of inherited wealth in the United States, 12 per cent (J.B. Davies, "The Impact of Inheritance on Lifetime Income Inequality in the United States", 1978, unpublished paper cited by Alan Harrison, *The Distribution of Wealth in Ten Countries*, p. 38). Inheritance is the main explanation for the greater inequality of wealth in Britain. Harbury and Hitchens concluded: "Inheritance is the major determinant of wealth inequality. Regression analysis attributed some two-thirds of the inequality in the distribution of wealth in 1973 to inheritance."

So how does inheritance operate? About 60 per cent of wealth passed on at death goes to the husband, wife or children of the deceased, and altogether nearly 90 per cent goes to relatives, including those outside the immediate family, according to the survey of estates left in 1973 carried out by the Royal Commission (Report No 5, p. 171). As you might expect, the larger the estate, the more likely it is that the deceased will give money to non-family, but even the largest estates gave 75 per cent to relatives.

Another important finding was that the practice of primogeniture — passing the bulk of family wealth to a single heir, the eldest male child — is still dominant among the rich. The sample was too small to draw firm conclusions, but twelve of the seventeen estates worth over £500,000 where there were two or more children gave more to one child than the other(s), whereas only seven of the twenty-one estates of between £15,000 and £50,000 did so. Where there were two children, the average division between them — when it wasn't equal — was 62/38 per cent. Overall, however, half of all bequests to two or more children were divided equally.

Generation-skipping is another pattern that is more common among the very rich. Partly this is to avoid tax (to prevent the same wealth being caught by death duties every generation, and to spread wealth more evenly in families), and partly because the very rich can afford to provide for more distant descendants. Less than a twentieth of the wealth in the sample passed to the grandchildren's generation or to younger relatives, and the Commission's survey only covered estates of those in the top 5 per cent of wealth holders. But for those with estates over £500,000, bequests to third or fourth generations were three times as likely. So only the very rich are likely to inherit when young.

The Grosvenors

The oldest model for a really rich dynasty is the Grosvenor family, whose current representative, Gerald Grosvenor, the sixth Duke of Westminster, is engaged in building up an international property development empire based on a trust structure. How little property-ownership in central London has changed since the post-war Labour government seemed to threaten the ancient aristocratic estates of Grosvenor, Portman, de Walden and Cavendish! The Grosvenors had to "sell Pimlico" in the 1950s to pay the estate duty bill on the death of the second Duke of Westminster. When the seventh Viscount Portman died in 1948 he left an estate valued at £10 million (£115 million in 1986 money), *three-quarters* of which had to be paid in death duties. To meet the tax bill the family sold Dorset Square and Crawford Street in 1951 and 1952. Death duties were at their heaviest ever in 1947 – 49, when estate duty at up to 75 per cent was accompanied by legacy and succession duty, payable by the inheritor, at rates of between 2 and 20 per cent depending on how closely you were related to the deceased. The Duke of Devonshire sold Devonshire House on Piccadilly to property developers. It seemed that time and taxes would fragment the great West End freehold empires. No such luck.

The Grosvenor wealth derives primarily from the dowry of Mary Davies, who married Sir Thomas Grosvenor in 1677, when she was twelve. The dowry included a stretch of marshland that is now Mayfair and Belgravia. Using that quintessentially British device, the ninety-nine-year lease — probably invented in 1661 by Lord Southampton (who developed Bloomsbury and gave his name to Southampton Row) — it was developed to provide town houses for the post-Restoration gentry. The land was leased on low "ground rent" to property developers who built houses and sold the leases, which then reverted to the family after ninety-nine years and new leases could be sold. In this way the Grosvenors came to own huge swathes of the most expensive properties on the Monopoly board, and still do despite estate duty, Capital Transfer Tax, the Leasehold Reform Act and supposedly progressive taxation.

The fact that estate duty once did squeeze the rich was illustrated in 1953, when the second Duke died and the family had to sell off much of Pimlico to pay a record £11 million in duty, worth over £100 million in 1986 terms. The family properties are nevertheless now commonly estimated to be worth around £2,000 million, a figure that hasn't been contested by the Duke.

The third, fourth and fifth Dukes did not pay anything like as much estate duty as their predecessor. Estate duty ceased to be effective mainly because clever lawyers found ways round it. In common with the rest of the aristocracy, *ancien* or *nouveau*, the main device for avoiding estate duty was the discretionary trust. The old method of generation-skipping, that of straightforward "settled property", was ruled out in 1914, when assets put in trust for heirs became taxable as part of the estate of the settlor when he or she died.

The discretionary trust gets round this by giving the trustees "discretion" as to whom to bestow settled assets on. Thus, if the trustees were relatives or close personal friends, they could be relied on to pass the wealth on to the settlor's heirs, but there would be nothing in law to say that the assets "belonged" to the heirs. This element of discretion — usually a fiction in practice — meant that when the settlor died, the trust's assets were not part of his or her estate for estate duty purposes, and any capital sums paid out of it by the trustees to the settlor's heirs would be completely free of tax. The use of trusts became widespread among the non-aristocratic rich in the 1960s, and "arguing with my trustees" is now a familiar feature of upper-class life.

After the death of the second Duke, according to the *Daily Mail*, "the reorganisation of the Grosvenor Estates began on a strictly commercial basis". This included contingency plans for tax exile in the event of a Labour government serious about redistributing wealth. "I will remain in England for as long as practically possible, because I like it here," the present Duke told the *Mirror* (10 July 1984). "But if the moment does come, as well it might, when the price is too high in terms of destroying one's business, I will go offshore."

At present the price of preserving the family "business" is modest, although value for money isn't always obtained. The Duke is unusual among the aristocracy in being a wholehearted supporter of Mrs Thatcher, and in 1985 provided Mr and Mrs Tebbit with a "good-sized family house, but not overly large" near the House of Commons. He also had legal fees to pay for hiring top QC Robert Alexander for his unsuccessful appeal to the European Court of Human Rights against the right of some leaseholders to buy the freehold of houses when their leases expire.

The Dukes of Devonshire

The Cavendish family were quicker on the uptake when it came to tax avoidance. It took only the election of a Labour government in 1945 to convince the tenth Duke that the family pile was threatened. The next year he turned over most of his property to a discretionary trust, the Chatsworth Settlement. All he had to do was live for three years in order to avoid death duties (the three year-period was to stop people avoiding tax by making "death-bed" gifts), but before the three years was up the government changed it to five years. And fourteen weeks before the five-year period had expired the Duke expired himself, aged only fifty. The resulting tax bill significantly diminished the Cavendish estate, and much of it had to be paid in kind: Hardwick House, two hundred Claud Lorrain drawings, a Van Dyck sketch book, paintings by Rembrandt and Rubens and two Holbein cartoons. This had a lasting effect on the present, eleventh, Duke.

The next challenge from a Labour government was met with a more professional response. The Duke says he took one look at the small print of the Capital Transfer Tax law when it was introduced in 1975 and said: "Two generations! That's all we'll last." But he took a more optimistic view in 1983, after several years of planning to put the family's famous seat, Chatsworth House in Derbyshire, into a charitable trust for ninety-nine years. The new tax meant that transfers in and out of the 1946 Settlement became taxable, so it became important to exploit the tax advantages of owning a bit of the national heritage. Works of art of national importance could, and still can, be exempted from Capital Transfer Tax, provided the public has access to them, and certain other conditions are met.

Simon Winchester commented in the *Sunday Times* (23 October 1983): "The ducal survival instinct, when pitted against mere ideology, won the day." The Duke himself, then a recent convert to the SDP, said smugly, "It would be foolish to say we are protected for all eternity, but for many decades, for certain." It took four years of careful lobbying and negotiations with the Treasury to produce the scheme to "protect" Chatsworth. The Duke says proudly in every interview he now gives that Chatsworth is saved for the nation, and that the taxpayer doesn't have to pay a penny towards its upkeep. This is both untrue, in that the cost of all tax concessions is borne by other taxpayers, and hypocritical, in that it was the Treasury's stipulation that it would only grant favoured tax status to Chatsworth on condition that it didn't receive any direct financial support from the government.

Because of this stipulation, the Duke had to get £750,000 out of the bank as well as selling a Poussin painting for £1.6 million and some books for £200,000 in order to endow the charity with enough to afford Chatsworth's running costs. The Duke and Duchess now live "above the shop" in twenty-five private rooms, paying a "market rent" — although how one calculates the market rent for half a stately home is something of a mystery.

The idea of a charitable trust to protect the family's stately home was borrowed from the Duke of Norfolk, who set up Arundel Castle Trustees Ltd as a charity in 1976, to hold the family's stately home in perpetuity for the public benefit; and from the Marquess of Exeter, who did the same for Burghley House in Lincolnshire on his death in 1981.

Although this was supposed to have secured Chatsworth and its treasures for ever, in 1983 the Duke of Devonshire's lawyer, Tim Burrows, estimated that the charitable trust needed another £500,000 to secure the future maintenance of Chatsworth House and its works of art. The Duke entered negotiations with the British Museum to sell sixty-nine Old Master drawings (including some by Leonardo and Rembrandt). The Museum offered £5.25 million, but the Duke said he wanted £5.5 million and offered the drawings to Christies, where in July 1984 he pulled off the "saleroom coup of the century" (*Daily Mail*) by selling them for £21.2 million. This raised £13 million after tax, which was payable because the drawings hadn't been "saved for the nation". In December 1985 another batch came up at Christies: more than three hundred Old Master prints were sold for £3.6 million "in order to keep up the works of art at Chatsworth". In 1986 it seemed to have become an annual event: another fourteen drawings were put up for £2.5 million.

Apart from Chatsworth, the Cavendish family still owns — mostly through trusts — three English landed estates — 38,000 acres in Derbyshire (including the 12,000 acres of Chatsworth's grounds), 30,000 acres at Bolton Abbey in Yorkshire and the 1,200-acre Compton Estate which owns much of Eastbourne. Under a separate settlement with Irish trustees the family also owns the Lismore Castle estate in County Waterford. The Duke also has two London homes, in Eaton Square, Belgravia, and Chesterfield Street, Mayfair.

Buccleuch

The Scott family, whose title goes back even before the Grosvenors and the Cavendishes to 1663, had an even earlier lesson in the rudiments of estate duty. The seventh Duke of Buccleuch died in 1935, five weeks before the three years were up after making over his estate, valued at nearly £1 million (£23 million in 1986 terms), to his son. As a result estate duty of an estimated £250,000 (worth £5.8 million now) was payable. The eighth Duke learnt this lesson, and passed most of the family wealth on to the present ninth Duke in the 1950s, when he was in his fifties. As a result, his personal estate was worth only £718,706 when he died in 1973 (£2.9 million in 1986 money). The *Daily Telegraph* estimated that this saved at least £8 million in estate duty, worth over £30 million today.[1]

The present Duke, a Tory MP between 1960 and 1973, has consistently defended the idea of hereditary great estates, of which his is — territorially — the greatest. He owns 250,000 acres, mostly in Scotland, but also 11,000 acres around Boughton House in Northamptonshire, another stately home, a castle and a palace. He has described himself as the largest private landowner in Europe, but he has angrily denied being the richest man in Scotland, and has consistently complained of the burden of taxes, which is responsible for breaking up family estates, whose owners had been "the traditional guardians of the heritage for five hundred years". In the *Sunday Times* (24 July 1977) he wrote: "Although we can still benefit from the deeds of ancestors whose lands covered almost all of Britain, such estates have been shrinking rapidly in recent years due to estate duty and taxation." And in a letter to the *Financial Times* (6 December 1978): "Taxation penalises development, discourages much-needed capital investment and is causing the rapid break-up of estates." However, there's still no sign of his estate suffering the same fate, although he has resorted to the usual devices of the aristocracy to bolster his wasting assets. On the death of his father, the ninth Duke started opening his stately homes to the public.

He inadvertently revealed that his landholdings alone were worth at least £50 million in 1984, when he protested at the *Sunday Times*'s valuation of him at £250 million. His denial was detailed enough to provide a rough estimate of his minimum wealth.

I suspect that your correspondent knew that I was in charge of over 250,000 acres, and had presumed that all acres are worth £1,000. In point of fact, regrettably over 80 per cent of our acres are tenanted hilltops with a value of nearer £100 an acre. A further 10 per cent is pretty middling land, while the remaining 10 per cent barely includes anything in grade one land. I hope therefore that you will help defend me from those left-wing politicians who want to bring about a wealth tax (*Sunday Times*, 28 October 1984).[2]

In January 1986 he told the *Express*: "Landowners are, in the main, only wealthy if they cease to be landowners." Fifty million being, in the main, a mere bauble compared with what the non-landed aristocracy has got.

Fitzalan-Howard

The present, seventeenth, Duke of Norfolk is a reluctant aristocrat, a good example of what happens when the hereditary principle is stretched like a cheese fondue. He inherited the title from a distant cousin in 1975: the sixteenth Duke had only four daughters, and so the already titled merchant banker Lord Beaumont came to the title as the great-great-grandson of the second son of the twelfth Duke. "Succeeding by death is a poor way of getting on," he said at the time. "It took no effort on my part to inherit the dukedom of

Norfolk and all the other titles that I have," he told the *Daily Telegraph* in May 1978. "But I am justly proud to have commanded the First Division of the British Army on the Rhine — as I had to work for that off my own back."

All the same, he took the Norfolk fiefdom by the scruff of the neck when he acceded. His first problem was an estate duty bill on the sixteenth Duke's £2.7 million estate (about £7.6 million in 1986 money), a figure that is more a tribute to tax avoidance than a valuation of the Fitzalan-Howard name. This was strikingly demonstrated when the new Duke sorted out the death duty bill in 1978 by selling a 125-year lease on part of the Strand office development, Arundel Great Court — for £11 million (around £21 million in today's terms). The Howard family has owned the land for four hundred years, and retains the freehold. If there are death duties in the year 2103, when the lease reverts, the Duke of Norfolk will be able to afford them.

Part of the death duty bill was settled when the Treasury accepted five paintings in lieu of taxes of £120,000. The paintings were allowed to remain in the family's stately home, Arundel Castle, which was the new Duke's second problem. The sixteenth Duke had decreed in his will that Arundel should be handed over to the National Trust, "or similar body". The new Duke had a row with the trustees of his predecessor's estate because the National Trust didn't want the "150-room Victorian gothic showplace" (John Armstrong, *Daily Telegraph* estates correspondent) unless the trustees handed over £600,000 to maintain it with. The trustees had offered £500,000 and were prepared to pay more to have it taken off their hands but, according to the Duke: "I wanted it handed over to an independent trust. I won; I always do" (*The Times*, 24 January 1983).

So in 1976 Arundel became a "gift for the public benefit" owned by a charitable trust — an "independent" company with the Duke himself as chairperson. This satisfied the recommendation of the Standing Committee on Museums and Galleries that "heritage objects" handed over in lieu of taxes ought to be allowed to remain in their "historic settings" even if this were a private house, as long as there is public access to them. The Duke rents a flat "at a commercial rate" in the Castle for his twice-weekly visits, but has four other homes, one of which, Carlton Towers in Yorkshire, was also opened to the public, in 1977.

The Vesteys

I've picked on these ancient aristocratic families not because they're typical of the super-rich in modern Britain, but because they demonstrate the resilience of determined dynasts. Their histories also illustrate the significance of estate duty, and the ways round it. Invented in 1894 by Sir William Harcourt, estate duty produced 29 per cent of Inland Revenue receipts in 1908/09, and was a significant source of revenue until the 1970s (although it accounted for a much smaller percentage of total receipts as income tax gradually became a "mass" tax; during the 1970s the revenue from death duties declined from 7 per cent to 1.5 per cent of receipts, even after the introduction of Capital Transfer Tax).

An example of how a more recent dynasty has retained its wealth and power during this century is the Vestey family, aristocratic but not ancient, having bought their peerage from Lloyd George in 1922. Their dynastic ambition, their royal connections and their lack of patriotism are much the same as any seventeenth-century creation, but their determination to avoid tax is probably unique.

The case of the Vesteys also illustrates how rapidly attitudes and media have changed since Mrs Thatcher came to power. It was only in 1980 that the *Sunday Times* carried a huge five-part exposé of the family's tax-dodging. The articles, the result of a six-month investigation by Phillip Knightley, provoked a substantial and largely hostile outcry. It's impossible to imagine the *Sunday Times* publishing such an investigation now, hard to imagine the *Observer* devoting so many resources to it, and the public response would now be much more ambivalent.

But 1980 was not the first time that the Vesteys attracted unfavourable publicity for tax avoidance, the family's central obsession. There was a furious row in 1922 when one of the dynasty's founding brothers, William, bought a peerage from Prime Minister Lloyd George for £20,000. King George V was unhappy at having to approve the recommendation for someone who had gone into tax exile in 1915 when the country was at war, and wrote an unusually sharp letter to his prime minister.

The original Vestey brothers, William and Edmund, made the family fortune out of refrigerating meat around the turn of the century. They were the first to exploit the technology for shipping meat from Argentina, Russia and China to feed the British masses. They used this advantage to keep out competition in the British market. Cold stores were expensive to build, and the Vesteys kept the rent they charged meat traders low enough to discourage other people from building them. They could afford not to make much money on warehousing meat in the UK by making money at a different stage of the chain. From foreign cattle to butcher's shop, the Vesteys owned the whole operation. They bought up land in Argentina and later Australia, owned a shipping line, Blue Star, owned the cold stores at both ends and a chain of retail butcher's shops, Dewhurst, all over Britain.

Tax avoidance on a major scale began for the Vesteys in 1915, in response to the wartime Budget of 1914, which brought British companies' foreign profits into the tax net and increased income tax and death duties. The Vesteys set up an American company, National Cold Storage, which paid the Vesteys' British company, Union Cold Storage, £224,000 a year for the use of all its non-UK assets. Under American law the profits of National Cold Storage couldn't be taxed because they went to its owners, the Vestey brothers, who didn't live in the United States. They had gone to live in Argentina, which at the time didn't have income tax.

But the Vesteys couldn't come back to live in the UK without paying at least some income tax. This was insufferable for William Vestey and, after the war, in 1919, he visited England to give evidence to the Royal Commission on Taxation. Trying to persuade them that it would be in the country's interest as well as his own if his family could live in the UK tax free, he only succeeded in getting up the Commissioners' noses. Asked if he was domiciled in the UK, he replied: "No. Buenos Aires. I am technically abroad at present, but I came over specially to appear before this Commission. The present position of affairs suits me admirably. I am abroad; I pay nothing." (Royal Commission evidence quoted by Knightley.)

This was too much for one Commissioner, who asked: "Are you not prepared to pay *anything* for the advantage of living here?" No answer. "With respect, I should like to have an answer." After an intervention from the chair — "You are prepared, of course, to pay income tax as a resident upon your income, are you not?" — William finally got out: "Yes, I think I must say so."

At that moment, no doubt, he realised what he must *say*, but it was obvious what he must *do*. William and his brother set up a dis-cretionary trust in Paris (the 1921 Paris Settlement) to receive the income from their business empire, which would be invested by the trustees, who were reliable family friends and who were well rewarded for their role. The income from these investments would then be allocated into two further trusts lasting for twenty-one years, one called "William's Fund" and the other "Edmund's Fund".

These trusts had a dual purpose. First, there was the dynasty; this way tax-free capital was preserved for the descendants of the two brothers. Secondly, the brothers were provided with tax-free sums on which they could live — in the UK. This was achieved, more or less, by simply ignoring British tax law. The person setting up a trust shouldn't be able to benefit from it, so the trustees of the Paris Settlement lent money to the Vesteys' new business vehicle, Western United Investment, which in turn acted as banker for William and Edmund and provided interest-free loans. To the lay person this might look like straight fraud, given that the "authorised persons" who "directed" the trustees in their investments were none other than William and Edmund; but the House of Lords found otherwise in an astonishing judgment in 1949.

This judgment was the culmination of the first attempt by the Inland Revenue to tax significantly any of the Vestey millions following William's death in 1940. The Revenue, in assessing death duties, found out about the Paris Settlement and demanded at least £6 million unpaid income tax (the present-day equivalent of over £100 million), arguing that the income of the Paris Settlement was effectively the brothers' income. This was accepted all the way up to the House of Lords. In the Court of Appeal, for instance, Lord Justice Somervell ruled: "The Vesteys were receiving a benefit in the shape of loans without interest. In my view the whole income of the trustees may be deemed the income of the Vesteys." But the House of Lords, stretching the meaning of the word pedantry, let alone the words of the statute, found that neither brother had an "individual" right to control the trust's income, since it was exercised jointly, nor did interest-free loans constitute "beneficial enjoyment" of that income. "Tax avoidance is an evil," said Lord Normand, with calculated hypocrisy, "but it would be the beginnings of much greater evils if the courts were to overstretch the language of the statute to subject to taxation people of whom they disapproved."

It's not as if William and Edmund weren't above a bit of sharp practice in order to defend their massive wealth without the House of Lords' assistance. In 1917 they lied to the Foreign Office, which was trying to get them to stop their American company shipping lard to neutral Norway for fear that it would be resold to the Germans. An official reported:

I have communicated with Messrs Vestey who say that beyond the fact that the American firm, which is a separate entity, holds shares in the London firm, there is no connection between them, and they are not in a position to control the actions of the American firm.

This was quite untrue.

In 1934, the Argentinian government set up a Commission to investigate allegations of price-fixing and profit-skimming against foreign meat businesses, primarily the Vesteys. They arrested Vestey manager Richard Tootell, who said that the production cost figures the Commission wanted were in London. The next day a Vestey ship was detained on a tip-off and twenty-one crates labelled "Corned Beef" were found to contain the Vestey business documents. But William was able to head off a joint Argentinian – British investigation of his business by insulting the Argentinians, who sought to sue for criminal libel, which in turn offended the Foreign Office.

The wealth of the Vesteys only returned to the public eye in the 1972 dock strike. The "shy millionaire" Sam Vestey was revealed as the ultimate owner of a company called Midland Cold Storage, which was at the centre of the crisis when four dockers were jailed by the Industrial Court for picketing it. The identity of the owner, although suspected by the workforce, was concealed by being registered incorrectly at Companies House in the name of the Ulster Bank.

"Many of our companies are in the ownership of nominees," explained Lord Vestey. "This is because we run a family business. Money is tied up in family trusts which cannot own companies and so we have to use nominees. It was purely a clerical error that the word nominees was missing from the Midland registration."

Vestey, pushed blinking into the limelight, explained the family's secretiveness: "For more than eighty years we have maintained a total silence about our affairs. We are, after all, a private business." Meanwhile the Inland Revenue began its second assault. A routine enquiry about Ronald Vestey's surtax return in 1967 led to the discovery of a series of payments of capital from offshore trusts to various members of the family. The structure of the tax avoidance arrangements had changed slightly. The original Paris Settlement had closed in 1942 and been succeeded by the "1942 Trust", the bank accounts of which were still in Paris, but the books were kept in

Uruguay by Vestey employee James Flynn. The other trustee was resident in Argentina. The annual income of the 1942 Trust was now divided equally between Samuel's Fund and Edmund's Fund, Lord "Sam" Vestey and his cousin Edmund being the respective heirs of the two founding brothers.

The Revenue tried to levy income tax on a series of payments totalling £2.6 million between 1962 and 1966 (worth around £16 million now), and lost the case in the House of Lords on slightly different arguments. This time it was argued that even if the trust income could be deemed to be the income of whoever set up the trust, it couldn't be the income of their heirs and successors. In ruling thus the Law Lords had to overturn one of their own previous judgments (*Congreve*, 1948). The Inland Revenue hadn't helped its case by demanding £274,121 each from Ronald Vestey's daughters, when they'd only received payments of £100,000 each. But the decision of the Lords was a second perverse and disgraceful verdict in favour of the Vestey family, and this time brought the law into disrepute. Although Chancellor Geoffrey Howe did nothing in his 1980 Budget about the loophole the House of Lords had created, the law was finally changed in the 1981 Budget after the outcry over the *Sunday Times* articles.

Since then the affairs of the Vestey family have retreated into comfortable obscurity again. They continue to live well in this country, while most of their money continues to accumulate outside it. Lord Sam is said to be quite happy with the new law, as the family has various other trust funds that Phillip Knightley never found out about. If he is still getting money into Britain tax-free, it's difficult to know how he's doing it, but he has more resources at his disposal than either the Inland Revenue or investigative journalists.

The statutory accounts of the Vestey's UK holding company, Union International, shed no light on the family's affairs. In the last year for which accounts have been filed at Companies House, dividends of £2.1 million were paid to the benefit of members of the Vestey family, presumably to trusts abroad. The company, which bought Baxters' 400 butchers shops in March 1985 and 170 Matthews shops in September 1986, then had a world turnover of £1,348 million, on which it succeeded in making a profit of only £11 million (less than 1 per cent of sales), and paying tax — all outside Britain — of just £2 million. The accounts explained: "UK corporation tax has not been provided in the current year as, after making the adjustments required for taxation purposes, there are no chargeable profits for the year."

The Business Aristocracy

The Vesteys are perhaps only the most blatant example, the avoidance of tax being a family obsession. It is a *dynastic* obsession, though, rather than an extension of personal greed: the original Vestey brothers, being notoriously frugal teetotallers, weren't interested in spending the money thus saved on themselves, although Lord Sam lives in the style to which such money has enabled him to become accustomed. Taxation is not the only threat to family businesses: businesses that are less international than the Vesteys' or not property-based like the Grosvenors' have the problem of investment, which means bringing in outside interests and diluting family control. Cadbury and Guinness are classic examples of family groups retaining a form of control over businesses after they ceased to have majority ownership. Until the merger with Schweppes in 1969, the Cadbury chocolate business was controlled by family members, and intermarried members of the Fry and Pascall families whose firms had been taken over. Even now, the Cadbury family has an influential holding, Dominic Cadbury is still chief executive and other family members are in managerial positions.

The descendants of Lord Iveagh, the founder of the "Guinnessty" intermarried over several generations with the Channon, Lennox-Boyd and Hamilton-Temple-Blackwood families, as well as the many branches of the original Guinness family. This family group still owns a substantial minority stake in the brewing company, and makes up half of its twelve-strong board. The overlapping shareholdings of these six members of the dynasty alone are worth a total of £30 million.

If we look at who the biggest business owners are (Table 6 on p. 136 shows a league table of dividends from large shareholdings in single companies), the inheritors — four Sainsburys, Forte junior and a Polizzi (Lord Forte's daughter) — appear to be outnumbered by those who built their own fortunes. Or rather, who organised other people building it for them.

Not all tycoons believe in the dynastic ideal. Gerald Ronson of Heron, the second largest private company in Britain after Littlewoods, says: "I've got no capital in the business. I'm not going to leave any to my children. They won't be short of a bob, but they won't have a big stake in Heron. I don't believe in it. I started with nothing."

TABLE 6

Top British Dividend Earners 1985/86[3]

	Company	
David Sainsbury	Sainsbury	£13,374,706
"Tiny" Rowland	Lonrho	£8,100,000
Sir Terence Conran	Storehouse	£4,481,853
Sir John Sainsbury	Sainsbury	£4,033,207
Sir Phil Harris	H. Queensway	£2,605,093
Rocco Forte	Trusthouse Forte	£2,293,560
Simon Sainsbury	Sainsbury	£2,023,214
Olga Polizzi	Trusthouse Forte	£1,868,437
Timothy Sainsbury	Sainsbury	£1,858,929
John Aspinall	Aspinall Hldgs	£1,289,269
Noel Lister	MFI	£1,082,288
Lord Forte	Trusthouse Forte	£1,019,492
Alan Sugar	Amstrad	£1,004,880

That's not strictly true. Heron is an abbreviation of his father's name, Henry Ronson, who owned a substantial furniture business, employing 350 people in 1956, when Gerald was seventeen. In that year Henry Ronson sold a factory he had built for £100,000 for £198,500, and father and son went into property development. Henry was chairperson of Heron until his death in 1974. The company is 100 per cent owned by Ronson family trusts. Sixty per cent is held by the Ronson Charitable Foundation, and the rest is "in trust", presumably for the benefit of his grandchildren. As the company doesn't pay dividends, his children must be provided for out of other personal wealth. All profits are ploughed back into the business, and according to Ronson the company is growing at 25 per cent a year. He pays himself "a good salary, enough to be comfortable", in fact one of the highest salaries in the country: £449,000 in 1985.

Because Heron doesn't pay dividends, Ronson doesn't feature in the business owners league table (Table 6), although he does appear in the salaries chart (Table 7).[4] But a comparison of the numbers in Tables 6 and 7 shows how much richer business owners are than business managers. The only name that appears in both Tables 6 and 7 is that of "Tiny" Rowland, chair and chief executive of Lonrho, once the "unacceptable face of capitalism". He finds it convenient —

TABLE 7

Top British Salaries 1985/86

	Company		Rise
William Brown	Walsham Bros	£1,268,583	46%
Ralph Halpern	Burton	£1,004,000	85%
Paul Plant	Burton	£710,000	77%
Laurence Cooklin	Burton	£705,000	78%
Robert Bauman	Beecham	£690,000	
A director	Robert Fleming	£509,000	
Stanley Kalms	Dixons	£487,654	134%
David Scholey	Mercury Secs	£478,000	
Gerald Ronson	Heron	£449,000	1%
Richard Ringwald	Laporte	£409,908	91%
"Tiny" Rowland	Lonrho	£392,285	22%
Sir John Nott	Lazard Bros	£366,436	100%
Frank Russell	Mansfield	£350,000	40%
Ernest Saunders	Guinness	£350,000	80%
Non-UK-resident directors			
Dick Giordano	BOC	£883,100	3%
Bryan Christopher	BSR	£380,000	-28%

Last column shows most recent annual pay rise.

since he owns the shares through companies based outside the UK — to take his pocket money in the form of a salary.

Managers can now become business (part-) owners through share option schemes. Several of the salaried class (Table 7) appear in Table 8 (p. 139), which shows the beneficiaries of the device by which they are accumulating major capital as opposed to income.

The biggest name to appear in both Tables 7 and 8 is salaried-manager turned tycoon Ralph Halpern, who made his name with Top Shop, a Burton subsidiary launched in 1961. He takes a stern view of certain forms of enterprise: "The courts should understand that stealing from shops is as serious as household burglary," he said in July 1986 (*Sunday Telegraph*, 6 July 1986), criticising magistrates for not giving heavy enough sentences. But he admits: "The ever-increasing attractiveness of shop displays and layouts does make it much easier for people to pick up goods without paying for them." His flair for increasing the attractiveness of shop displays powered his rise from trainee manager to general manager, and made him a highly poachable commodity. When Woolworth was taken over by a consortium he was approached and asked to be chief executive, but it was an offer he could refuse. "I was offered £65,000 a year and membership of BUPA," he said to the *Observer* (21 July 1985). "I told them they would have to offer significant stock incentives."

Just what Halpern means by "significant" becomes clear in Table 8, and Woolworth's new owners obviously took what he said to heart, because the "stock incentive" they offered to the person who eventually took the job is the most valuable share option scheme listed in that table. John Beckett — brother of former CBI Director General Sir Terence — took the Woolworth job, and his share options were worth £7.3 million by the time he retired in March 1986, whereas Halpern's Burton options were worth £5.6 million (£1.7 million of which he cashed in in February 1986). On the other hand John Beckett made do on a salary of £114,000, while Halpern's salary in 1985 was then the highest of any known UK-resident at £542,000, and was to become the best-known to reach the £1 million mark. His was in fact the second million-plus salary, but it coincided with tabloid revelations of his "five times a night with a topless model" and a row over a new £2.5-million option scheme.

Several managers, especially in retailing, have already cashed in share option profits of millions. Glen Renfrew, managing director of Reuters news agency and electronic information supplier, made a total profit of over £6 million in 1985 – 86. He began as a reporter in 1952, so there's hope for us all. The managerial route seems the most promising for acquiring "self-made" wealth. But are there any genuinely "self-made" business owners, people whom the Conservatives are always talking about who have launched their own business and built it up from nothing? Here are two.

Alan Sugar
The Hackney-bred descendant of a Polish great-grandfather in the clothing trade, Alan Sugar started selling car-radio aerials at a 100 per cent mark-up in a North London Saturday market instead of being an Education Department statistician. He formed Amstrad (Alan Michael Sugar Trading) in 1968 selling plastic turntable covers, and in 1975 made his first visit to Japan, "to plunder the technology".

The company was launched on the stock market in 1980, when he was thirty-three, selling a quarter-share of the business for £2 million. "I know where my roots are," he said then. "My family are

TABLE 8

Top Share Option Profits to 1987

	Company	Potential profit
John Beckett	Woolworth	£7,323,328
Glen Renfrew	Reuters	£6,164,858*
Alec Monk	Dee Corp	£6,027,338
Victor Monk	Charterhouse	£5,777,400
Ralph Halpern	Burton	£5,551,041*
William Wyllie	BSR Internatl	£3,300,000
Paul Plant	Burton	£2,679,711
Laurence Cooklin	Burton	£2,515,778
Michael Wood	Burton	£2,390,690*
Lord Hanson	Hanson Trust	£2,239,636*
Geoffrey Mulcahy	Woolworth	£2,163,142
Colin Brown	Woolworth	£2,080,239
Richard Harker	Woolworth	£2,080,239
Stanley Kalms	Dixons	£2,063,209

*Some or all profit already realised. [5]

still working class people." He was asked what he spent the money on. "Oh clothes," he said, vaguely, without the slightest interest. "Clothes and gadgets and trinkets and toys, video cameras, calculators that sing song, spelling machines for the kids. The point is, I've got to the top of the greasy pole and all I can do is forge ahead — it's in my nature."

The company made a profit then of £1 million. The figure for 1986 was £52 million, mainly because of Amstrad's successful word-processing computer for the price of an expensive typewriter. In May 1986, he sold 5 million shares when the price reached 520p, netting £26 million before he was forty. He was left with a share worth, at the last count, £340 million. An accountant who specialises in personal tax guesses that Sugar owns his shares through an offshore trust or company, quite possibly in Guernsey or the Isle of Man, in which case he doesn't have to pay his Capital Gains Tax bill (30 per cent of most of the £26 million, or nearly £7.8 million) until he brings the money back into this country.

He still lives in Chigwell, Essex, although his house is large. He also has a second home in Florida, so he could retire there and never pay the £7.8 million. To avoid paying Capital Gains Tax he would have to cease to be resident and "ordinarily resident" in the UK, which means in practice three complete tax years abroad. So he could just spend three years in America, saying he was going to break into the United States market, and then come back to Chigwell to retire, bringing his offshore pile with him tax free, or investing it in America depending on how he felt about the then Labour government. Even in 1985, his mother and father were worrying about him a lot. "It's difficult for them to comprehend what's going on and they cannot understand because they're factory workers and not business people. They're still concerned that all this is just a flash in the pan." He wears gold, has monogrammed shirts, a Rolls Royce Silver Cloud and a private aeroplane. His three teenage children go to private schools because the comprehensive system is not what it was when he was young, and he thinks Mrs Thatcher is wonderful. "She's done an excellent job for business and the country, but unfortunately 70 per cent of the population don't understand that. She's getting a raw deal" (*Today*, 13 April 1986).

Sugar is contemptuous of his business competitors and of British snobbery. At the launch of his IBM-imitation computer in 1986 he said he couldn't understand why other people didn't do what he'd done, making mass-market products at competitive prices. Any idea why they didn't? "Not really," he replied. "Perhaps they're more interested in finding out which class of seat they're sitting in on their trip to visit their Paris subsidiary."

Frank Russell

Frank Russell was paid a salary of £350,000 in 1985, the fifth highest salary published in company accounts that year. He is chairperson of Mansfield Originals, a private company in the ladies' coat and suit business, with total sales in 1985 of only £6 million. Pre-tax profit was £522,628.

Russell, sole owner and chairperson, paid himself £350,000 in salary and his joint managing director Barry Hancock £44,750. The company paid £378,400 in pension contributions for the two of them. In 1985 Frank declared a dividend of £2.80 per share. He owns all but one of the 75,000 shares, so that's £299,996. Oh, and he forgot to pay a dividend in 1984, so he declared £1.87 for that year and paid that too: another £200,354. Assuming most of the pension contributions were his own, Frank Russell took around £1,185,000 out of the business in the financial year to June 1985. There is clearly more to Mansfield than meets the eye. But not much more. Mansfield Originals is at the centre of a group of small companies whose total turnover is only about £10 million a year. When I told Russell he appeared to have the fifth highest salary in the country, Russell said: "Oh, I'm disappointed."

Mansfield coats, which have a high reputation, are sold in in-store "concessions" in department stores, including Harvey Nichols, under the Mansfield and Cache d'Or labels for between £198 and £230. The Mansfield company secretary described them as "not the very top end of the market — for the upper-middle class; you could afford them if you saved up for a year."

Russell built the group up from being a contract tailor off Commercial Street in the East End in 1954; now he's in his sixties and wants to enjoy life a little. He has endowed a scholarship in design at the Royal College of Art, but won't say what else he spends his money on. He has a flat on Hampstead Heath. He describes his business approach as "not really adventurous", the company as "very solid", says he's never borrowed money and his growth is slow. "We've always sold more than we can manufacture. We don't grow, we refine." So why does Frank Russell think he's entitled to such a large amount of money? The question does not make sense. "It's my company. I'm the sole owner. I've always been careful with money, but recently I've relaxed a bit."

Frank Russell is an example of the inconspicuous rich — only visible because, like the rest of the business aristocracy, he's required by company law to disclose certain of his finances.

Discreet new wealth

What are the sources of new wealth for those out of the headlines and the league tables? Growing businesses, especially in the service sector and when launched on the Unlisted Securities Market (the "junior" Stock Exchange). There have been five hundred millionaires launched on the Unlisted Securities Market in the five years between November 1980, when it was set up, and June 1986, according to accountants Touche Ross. It's misleading to say the USM has "created" millionaires: it's only a market, providing the owners of small businesses with a way of cashing in on some of their success.

Miles Halford of Touche Ross estimates that 60 per cent of the money raised by USM flotations goes back into the business, which leaves 40 per cent to be taken in cash by the person who (usually) set up the business. Only forty-four of the five hundred raised £1 million or more in cash on flotation — the rest had holdings and/or cash valued at a total of £1 million.

Even more discreetly, though, the spread of home ownership means that over half the population now have durable assets and have joined the bequeathing classes. Probably for the first time, it's now possible to get rich by saving — or at least, by your parents' saving. Houses are a peculiar form of wealth, in that they are heavily subsidised by the tax system, but can't be realised until you die or make alternative living arrangements.

A family's ability to preserve, augment and pass on wealth depends partly on the durability of the form their wealth takes. Property and land are durable, businesses and shops aren't, hence the tendency of new money to "go county" in one or two generations. The heirs of the founder of a business are never necessarily the best people to run it, but you can't go seriously wrong with property, shares or very old paintings.

Although Gerald Ronson of Heron may not have specific ambitions to build a dynasty, he doesn't want his descendants to sink straight back into the levelling mass. Families rise and fall, and in the meantime try to hang on for as long as possible. The length of their "hanging on", and the diversity and accessibility of sources of new wealth, are critical factors in determining how unequal a society will be.

---

1. *Daily Telegraph*, 8 April 1974.

2. If we take 80 per cent at £100 an acre, 10 per cent at £400 an acre and 10 per cent at £800, it comes to £50 million.

3. Directors' estimated dividend income, before tax, based on total dividend for period of latest annual accounts. UK dividends are paid with tax paid at 27 per cent; the figures in Table 6 are stated in pre-tax form. Final dividends are paid after the accounts date, so it is assumed that directors retain the latest holding declared in the accounts.

4. Table 6 also doesn't include many of the second and subsequent generation business élite inheritors who have diversified their investments.

5. Potential gain from share options is calculated using the share price at its 1986/87 high. Where options are (assumed to be) granted under the "tax efficient" provisions of the 1984 Finance Act the total shows the profit as if it were to be paid in taxed salary. Sources: Company accounts and Stock Exchange *Weekly Official Intelligence*.

10. TRICKS WITH TAX

> "We pay the highest rate of tax at the lowest level
> of income of any country in the EEC." — Mrs
> Thatcher, Leader of the Opposition, 29 March
> 1977. Later: "Every Conservative government
> gets taxes down." — Geoffrey Howe, Shadow
> Chancellor, 7 April 1979. Much later: "I feel that
> we owe quite a debt to the people in the bottom
> half. We have taken in my view too high a
> proportion of their income in tax." — Mrs
> Thatcher, *Panorama*, 17 February 1986.

What can be learnt from the record of past Labour governments?
The Attlee government's achievements in reducing material inequality in Britain were immense, and the creation of the welfare
state has now assumed a quasi-mythical quality. But the achievements of the Wilson/Callaghan governments have been underestimated, and it's surprising given the ferocity of the Thatcherite
reaction that they haven't been seen in a more favourable light. Part
of the explanation might be that the 1964–70 and 1974–79 governments didn't really know what they were doing, and if they achieved
greater equality this was almost despite themselves.

Wealth — among the richer half of the population — was gradually
becoming distributed more equally, through no particular fault of
either Labour or Conservative governments. Although Labour
governments strove to equalise incomes — through incomes policies
for those in work and higher benefits for those out of it — their main
achievements were building on the foundations of the collective
provision of the welfare state, which certainly led to greater equality
of condition, if not money income or wealth.

The 1964–70 Labour government
Harold Wilson set out the task with admirable clarity.

> Given a Labour victory, the test is this: will there be, twelve
> months from now, a narrowing of the gap between rich and poor,
> quite apart from any general upward movement there may be as
> the result of increased production? The answer is, quite simply,
> that there will.

That, unfortunately, was before the 1960 election (in the *New Statesman* of 3 October 1959). Before the Labour victory in the 1964 election, there was no such clear-headed manifesto. It was nevertheless taken for granted by all who were supporters of the 1964–70 Labour government that one of·its main tasks was to redistribute income and wealth from rich to poor.

Apart from the steady equalising of wealth, which was hardly a particularly conscious policy, the first Wilson government didn't diminish inequality in any significant respect except by the introduction of comprehensive education. It raised the real value of welfare benefits which, to its consternation, had the unintended effect of providing ammunition for the "poverty lobby", as more people could now be defined as below a higher "official poverty line". The poverty lobby came into being under the Conservatives but grew in voice and influence because of its connections in the Labour government. In order to attack the tardy and unenthusiastic moves by the Wilson administration to tackle the problems of family poverty, the new lobby used the higher Supplementary Benefits as the "official poverty line" in place of the old National Assistance scales. Peter Townsend, for instance, wrote an article in *The Times* headlined "A Million More in Poverty since 1966" (10 March 1971).

Social security benefits *did* lag marginally behind the growth in average earnings between 1966 and 1971 (although not since 1964).[1] Hence overall income inequality, in terms of the ratio of the bottom to the average, did not improve. The poor were better off under Labour, but so were Mr and Mrs Average, and Mr Rich, and the differences between them all were proportionally as unequal as ever.

Michael Stewart, a Wilson government adviser, did not conceal his disappointment at the government's failure to bring in a wealth tax in *The Labour Government's Economic Record 1964–70*:

> There has been a good deal of talk about a wealth tax in Labour circles during the two or three years before the 1964 election, and Mr Callaghan, then Shadow Chancellor and subsequently Chancellor for Labour's first three years in office, appeared to view it with some sympathy. [But] nothing was done. Indeed there is no evidence that it was ever considered as a serious possibility by most senior members of the government, and although the heavy burden placed on the Inland Revenue by other tax reforms may have played a part in this, it can hardly have been

the principal reason, for there was no mention of a wealth tax in the 1964, 1966 or 1970 election manifestos. Conviction, rather than feasibility, appears to have been the missing ingredient (p. 84).

Nor was the Labour government to do anything new about the transfer of wealth, and in particular inheritance. The only change was an increase in 1968 in the "deathbed" period to catch lifetime gifts, from five to seven years. In 1986 Nigel Lawson took us back eighteen years to this position, where you now have to survive for seven years after making a gift of more than £90,000 to avoid tax on it.

The only substantial advance in taxing the rich came at the start of the administration with the introduction of Capital Gains Tax in 1964. James Callaghan, Chancellor of the Exchequer, announced its introduction on 11 November 1964:

> This measure [Capital Gains Tax] will bring to end the state of affairs in which hard work and great energy are fully taxed while the fruits of speculation and passive ownership escape untaxed. This is part of fair play between groups of taxpayers.

The Conservatives had brought in a "short-term gains tax" in response to concern about property speculators in 1962, which taxed capital gains if they were realised (that is, if the asset is sold) within six months. The revenue was negligible. Capital Gains Tax was a heavier tax: gains realised in the first year were taxable at the taxpayer's top income tax and surtax rates, or 30 per cent thereafter. The Heath government made it 30 per cent only and the 1974—79 Labour government left it unchanged, perhaps because inflation had already made it a patently unfair tax — it taxed the gains on assets whose prices had gone up simply because of inflation.

The 1964—70 Labour government did nothing about income tax, allowing inflation to push more low-paid workers into the tax net while those higher up the scale got pushed into the surtax bracket (nowadays roughly equivalent to higher-rate income tax). Stewart says "the overall effect of all this must have been progressive", and it wasn't realised until the mid-1970s what an unprogressive disaster it had been (p. 160). We are now so used to discounting the effects of inflation almost automatically in all money calculations that it's difficult to understand the slowness of policy makers and commentators in realising the effects of inflation on the tax system.

The 1974–79 Labour government

Things were very different in 1974. Everywhere, the political Right was on the defensive. Michael Meacher wrote a large, confident piece in the *New Statesman* called "The Coming Class Struggle" (4 January 1974). He can have little realised how unequal that struggle was going to be. The demoralisation of the Right was demonstrated by the reply from Peregrine Worsthorne, now editor of the *Sunday Telegraph*, in the following issue ("The Politics of Envy"), in which he argued that although pursuing social justice was morally right, it was not wise in practice. He could only argue that people were less likely to be envious of that which they know little about, and that the purpose of conservatism is to propagate "acceptance of, and resignation to, the human condition", *viz* inequality.

But this was not how Keith Joseph, shortly to launch Mrs Thatcher on an unsuspecting Tory party, saw it. His brand of Toryism boldly swept aside social justice as secondary to the "creation of wealth" and the nurturing of the tender entrepreneurial plant:

> The entrepreneur takes risks; which means that he [sic] has a particular temperament; he is sensitive to demand, which often means to people. He is born, not made, but can easily be unmade, discouraged (*New Statesman*, 18 April 1975).

Michael Meacher had said, "correctly", as Marxist monographs would have it, "we are now witnessing the steady breakdown of the post-war settlement between capital and labour". But the breakdown was to be to the advantage of the former not the latter. "Meacherism" reached its apogée simultaneously with the election of Mrs Thatcher as Tory leader, when Barbara Wootton delivered a lecture at the London School of Economics called "The Last Days of Capitalism" in May 1975 (*New Statesman*, 6 June 1975). This unlikely epitaph epitomises the two crucial weaknesses of socialist economics — incomes policy and tax — in one unworkable scheme.

> A limit should be set on the annual increase of personal incomes in such a way that the total should not exceed the increase in ... output. This would apply alike to speculators, pensioners, shareholders and the self-employed, as well as to wage-earners, the principle being that the larger your income, the less you would be able to add to it ... and above a not very high level of personal income no advance at all would be permitted. The simplest

method of operating such a policy would be to subject anyone who succeeded in getting more than his [sic] entitlement to a 100 per cent tax on the illegitimate excess. In my view such a policy could and should be applied now.

This was typical of the dominant but brittle rhetoric of the "official Left", by which is meant something different from both Labour Party and Labour government policy. It was this kind of rhetoric that genuinely struck fear into the hearts of the business interest, which was and is not necessarily naturally Thatcherite. It also, less genuinely, allowed the new Right to incite a climate of opinion in which the Conservative party was able to appropriate the word "freedom".

Baroness Wootton's 100 per cent tax rate was not just a proposal, it was two percentage points away from fact. The 98 per cent top tax rate on unearned income had no effect at all on inequality, while playing straight into the Right's hands in the propaganda battle.

Apart from the immediate gain of a 30 per cent increase in pensions in July 1974 (which resulted in a once-and-for-all real gain of over 10 per cent in pension purchasing power), the 1974–79 Labour government made two significant steps forward in the direction of greater equality in the longer term. In 1975, it brought in Capital Transfer Tax and the State Earnings-Related Pension Scheme (SERPS). Capital Transfer Tax was a response to the fact that the rich had found ways round estate (death) duty through the use of discretionary trusts and passing wealth on more than seven years before death. It taxed all transfers of wealth during an individual's lifetime, and brought in a ten-yearly charge on discretionary trusts. Although the lifetime transfer rates were low, and there were still plenty of exemptions, in time it would have raised a considerable amount of revenue. It was weakened and then abolished by the Conservatives before this could happen. Much the same fate befell SERPS, although it survives for the time being. It too had drawbacks, in that the "earnings-related" element perpetuated unequal earned incomes into retirement, but it was an advance on what went before.

The 1974–79 Labour government is constantly reviled by the Left for its many failures, although it's often forgotten that it only had a majority for two years, from the second 1974 election, in October, to the by-elections which Labour lost in Walsall North and Workington in November 1976. Liberal leader David Steel had announced his willingness to work in coalition at the Llandudno conference in September, and when Denis Healey's Budget was voted down in March 1977, the Lib–Lab pact was wheeled into place. It had become necessary the month before when Labour leftwingers antagonised the fourteen Scottish and Welsh nationalists by scuppering the devolution bills in parliamentary committee. The IMF crisis in September 1976 had already destroyed what desire James Callaghan might have had to attack the power structures sustaining inequality. But the Lib–Lab pact provided the excuse: unlike Wilson's minority government in May to October 1974, Callaghan's last eighteen months before the Winter of Discontent were characterised by political cowardice.

Tax Avoidance

To get to grips with why decades of allegedly progressive taxation had so little effect on the distribution of after-tax incomes, we need to know a few of the "tricks with tax" which mean that all is not what it seems. The Conservatives like to imply that all tax avoidance is jobbing builders doing work for cash and claiming the dole. John Biffen once implied that unemployment and growth figures weren't as bad as they seemed because really the whole nation was thriving on the skive. "The hidden ready cash economy is well and flourishing and is nationwide," he said, pointing to some of the more extravagant estimates of the size of the underground economy — up to 15 per cent of economic activity (Conservative Central Office press release, 19 April 1985).

Serious examinations of the underground economy, such as that by Stephen Smith (*Britain's Shadow Economy*, 1986), suggest that it accounts for only 3 – 5 per cent of national income. Smith also points out that wilder claims actually make it harder to collect taxes: people are less likely to pay tax if they believe everyone else gets away with evasion. The fact is that if tax evasion and the underground economy have grown in recent years it's because of Conservative dogma about reducing civil service numbers, which has cut staff at the Inland Revenue by 14,500 between 1979 and 1986. As the Inland Revenue union never ceases to point out, and the government never pays a blind bit of notice, investigation staff at the Revenue return to the taxpayer four times their salary in illegally evaded tax. For every £1 spent on combating tax evasion and avoidance, £27 of unlawfully unpaid tax was collected in 1985.

This comes mainly from rich taxpayers with financial advisers (with whom the Revenue is often too understaffed to argue), rather than the Tories' archetypal working-class scrounger. But the focus of the Revenue's investigation work is on "moonlighters" and "ghost" workers, that is, the bottom end. In 1985, the government allowed the Revenue not to cut staff by as much as planned so that 180 people could be redeployed to deal with moonlighting and ghosts.

The Revenue examines just 3 per cent of all unincorporated businesses (that is, the self-employed) and only 1 per cent of companies — yet in 91 per cent of cases challenged, extra tax is collected, and in half these cases extra penalties and/or interest are collected, indicating a more serious level of criminal evasion. On the other hand, checks on the PAYE system — which covers most ordinary employees — discovered "irregularities" in only one-third of cases selected, and yielded only £5.50 per £1 spent. [2]

What's more, the civil service union CPSA claims that £160 million a year extra VAT could be collected each year if the government were prepared to take on another 1,700 Customs officials — and that's the clear gain for the taxpayer after paying their salaries, but not counting the savings in social security payments to 1,700 people on the dole. Most of the extra revenue is undeclared VAT on the basis of government figures showing that each VAT control officer discovers undeclared tax amounting to £122,750, but some of it would be raised by the collection of VAT due from identified debtors that Customs doesn't have the staff to visit. [3]

Tax Fiddles

The unpopularity and tedium of taxation is immensely useful to the rich. The fact that "no one likes paying tax" means that the promise of tax cuts seems like a good idea and makes public attitudes to tax avoidance ambivalent. Hostility to "the taxman" does the ruling class's work for it. Opinion surveys of attitudes to dishonesty regularly show almost no disapproval for people failing to declare income to the Revenue. Partly this must the result of successful Tory propaganda about Britain being a heavily-taxed nation, whereas in fact, taking all taxes and social security contributions together the UK has the lightest burden of any of the major West European economies — despite its increasing from 38 to 44 per cent of national income in Mrs Thatcher's first four years alone. [4]

Tax avoidance is constantly incited by the millionaires' press. Take for just one instance Patrick Cosgrave in the *Daily Telegraph* (proprietor: millionaire Conrad Black):

The tax exile is generally held in abhorrence by politicians, principally Labour politicians, but often Tories as well. The rancorous note of envy has been echoed by many journalists. The pretence is made that the departing rich are not merely fortunate (if he [sic] has inherited wealth) or gifted (if he has made it), but, somehow, unpatriotic, or lacking in public spirit. It is all balderdash (6 June 1986).

Cosgrave goes on to explain why he'd be "on the next flight out of the country" if one of his novels became a blockbuster. "It would be because I could not be sure that I could do the same trick again. I would want to take the opportunity to provide financially for myself and my family." Ah, the conservatives' touchstone again: the family. It doesn't matter how iniquitous, how greedy, how unpatriotic, how unwilling to contribute to the general welfare (all incidentally denied) the citizen is, as long as he's doing it for his (sic) family. It's but a small step from here to feeling sorry for Aldo Gucci, patriarch of the fashionable Italian leather family firm, locked up at the age of eighty-five in New York for illegally evading at least $7.4 million in US taxes. (Mind you, on that occasion the family was Aldo's downfall, as it was his estranged son Paulo's loose talk which led to the tax investigation in the first place.)

Fiddling the Inland Revenue is not a game in which all players are equal. The more money you've got, the more you save by cheating the tax collector. The unpopularity of the Inland Revenue is so widespread through all levels of society that its inspectors have to behave cautiously and politely. The heaviest attack they have ever launched, on Rossminster's tax avoidance business in 1979, involved dawn raids to seize papers relating to a whole series of schemes that turned out not to be legally effective in avoiding tax — yet the outcry against such an invasion of privacy and attack on the civil liberties of a collection of rich business people and MPs was so great that an operation of its kind hasn't been attempted since.

The contrast with the behaviour of enforcement authorities in other departments, dealing with poor people, is striking. The DHSS claims control squads, for instance, are regularly engaged in dawn raids on Supplementary Benefit claimants to discover whether they are living with someone or whether they've got a job on the side. The Employment Department's "Rabbit" squads perform a similar role in relation to people claiming unemployment benefit.

On the other side of the fence, taxpayers are often allowed to estimate their expenses, for instance, and the Inland Revenue won't bother to challenge the estimate unless it's obviously a try-on, *and* is over a certain figure — below which it's not considered worth the inspector's time. Only the Inland Revenue is explicitly allowed to ignore the law when convenient for it and its clients: there are a number of published "extra-statutory concessions" — meaning things which the Inland Revenue by custom and practice doesn't bother to enforce or clarify by taking to court, but which aren't covered by an Act of Parliament.

A constant guerilla war is being conducted in secret between the Inland Revenue and the rich, or at least their advisers. The propaganda of the rich portrays "the taxman" as a threat to us all. In fact, the real battles are over obscure points of law, and the Inland Revenue's stance is that of a very urbane guerilla. Much of the battle in the courts is like a word game, with thousands of pounds depending on whether sums are "income" or "capital".

To take one small recent example, a "defeat" for the Revenue: the case of Mrs Henwood in 1985. Mrs Henwood was one of several beneficiaries of a discretionary trust set up by a Joseph Levy in 1961. The trustees of the fund paid a total of £114,250 to Mrs Henwood, not as "income" but as "advances out of capital".[5] The courts agreed that these advances weren't income, and Mrs Henwood got her £114,250 completely tax-free, instead of paying up to 75 per cent income tax on it (15 per cent unearned income surcharge, abolished in 1984, plus 60 per cent depending on how much other income she was already getting). She may have saved as much as £85,688 — which would have paid for home helps for a half-day a week for a year for 134 old people.

Rossminster

This is the tax avoiders' government: the significance of the Rossminster affair in the 1970s was that so many prominent Tory politicians were involved (John Nott provided "consultancy", Peter Rees QC gave counsel's opinions, Tom Benyon MP was a director, Peter Walker used the company for financial advice). Rossminster Bank was the market leader in what was becoming known as the tax-avoidance "industry". Highly elaborate schemes were sold "off the shelf" to rich customers, by which they could reduce their tax bills by exploiting tax relief on business loans and any other loopholes its accountants and lawyers could find. The operation was killed off by Inland Revenue harassment and a series of legal judgments which ruled out one scheme after another. A Tory government committed to tax cuts for the rich, however, is the continuation of Rossminster's activities by other means.

The Tory argument is that Rossminster's tax avoidance schemes were *caused* by the "confiscatory" levels of taxation under the Labour government. Former Tory Treasury minister Jock Bruce-Gardyne says: "Highly complex avoidance schemes in the 1970s were the offspring of confiscatory taxation." Benyon says: "A lot of people got very frightened about what Healey was saying. The service we were offering, avoidance within the law, caught the imagination of people." (Quoted by Nigel Tutt, *The Tax Raiders: The Rossminster Affair*.) The solution, then, according to Bruce-Gardyne, is to "reduce the confiscatory nature of marginal rates, then the cause of such schemes is diminished". This is what the government has done.

Defenders of Rossminster like to point out the difference between (legal) tax avoidance and (illegal) tax evasion, and to stress that Rossminster was very carefully and properly in the avoidance business. Roy Tucker and Ron Plummer, the men behind Rossminster, complain that the Inland Revenue never filed charges after a "dawn raid" on their homes on (Revenue officials *do* have a sense of humour) Friday, 13 July 1979. But there is no hard and fast distinction between avoidance and evasion, as their lordships discovered when various controversial tax cases went to the House of Lords.

The curious thing about the Rossminster affair is that none of Rossminster's clients ever saved any tax through the firm's imaginative tax avoidance schemes. The effect of stretching tax law to its limits was to provoke the Law Lords in the *Ramsay* and *Furniss* decisions in 1981 and 1984 to invent the doctrine of "artificiality" — which holds that anything done simply and solely to avoid tax, without any commercial or other purpose and effect, can be ignored by the Inland Revenue. Hence tax avoidance pure and simple is deemed illegal, and the same as tax evasion, while "ordering one's affairs in such a way as to minimise tax" is still legal, a precedent established by the *Duke of Westminster* case in 1935.

Tax havens
One of the loopholes Rossminster did succeed in exploiting was the use of offshore parts of the country. Guernsey doesn't have passport control, because for most purposes it's part of the UK. The two main

purposes for which it isn't part of the UK are tax and company law. Company accounts in Guernsey are not filed for inspection by the public. Income tax in Guernsey is 20 per cent, and corporation tax is a flat £300 for companies whose business is not carried out in Guernsey and which aren't controlled there. Which brings us to the "Sark Lark", described by Nigel Tutt in *The Tax Raiders*.

There is a regular boat service on the nine-mile journey to the small island of Sark from St Peter Port harbour in Guernsey. In the summer, tourists flock to make the trip and the boats are packed. Among the crowd it is still possible to make out an accountant or solicitor with his client making the trip too. These professional men can even be spotted wearing T-shirts, shorts and training shoes to take advantage of the midsummer weather, but their leather briefcases mark them out as part of the "Sark Lark". Once the boat is under way, the professional hoists his briefcase to his knees and out come his papers. Holding directors' meetings away from Guernsey, such as in Sark, meets the criteria for paying just £300 a year in tax. With a quorum of non-Guernsey directors, "control" is outside Guernsey. Some don't even bother to land in Sark, conducting business on the boat such as an accountant discussing share dealing with a client and signing documents. When the boat arrives in Sark, the businessmen often jump across to the next boat leaving and are back in Guernsey in another forty minutes. Some have their photos taken on the Sark quay for the taxman [sic].

Some of the Rossminster schemes were more elaborate. A number of Sark residents were signed up as directors of companies handling sums as large as £150 million. Martin Joyner, who ran a photographic and fancy-goods shop on Sark told Tutt:

I was on the board of a dozen companies at the most. It paid for convent schooling for my girl in Guernsey. We were assured that everything was done properly. It started at about £50 and was never more than £80 for each company per year. The most I made was £3,000 at the peak. I got the feeling others did better. Some went for long lunch parties.

Jersey

According to *Tatler* (February 1986), fifty or so millionaires apply each year to become tax exiles on Jersey, but only twelve on average get in. They have to prove an income of £50,000 a year, buy an approved house costing £250,000 or more, and pass scrutiny by the Economic Adviser's Office to ensure they are "community-minded and crashingly respectable".

Lord Villiers, commodity broker and heir of the Earl of Jersey, says: "The tax haven label is unfair. It's just that we run our financial affairs better than on the mainland. There hasn't been this great radical feeling we must reform everything." Gerald Durrell, one of several authors on the island also thinks the tax haven label is unfair. "Coming here had nothing to do with tax," he says. Nothing at all to do with 20 per cent income tax and duty-free goods. "All that was a pleasant surprise. As a matter of fact, I paid English tax my first six years here."

Harry Patterson, better known as Jack Higgins, the author of *The Eagle Has Landed*, takes a different line. "I don't think it's morally wrong to become a tax exile," he says. But he doesn't like the islanders much, partly because he became a social outcast since his divorce. "One of the awful things about being rich and successful," he told a radio interviewer in 1986, "is that you are forced into the company of rich people, who really are an undesirable class of people." Particularly those on Jersey: "The point of people here is that money is all they have. Imagine what it's like to spend most of your life with some fellow who's made his money out of super-markets, or a bore like Alan Whicker."

Or even the inventor of the Black and Decker Workmate, South African Ron Hickman, who has spent £1.3 million building his stu-pendously tasteless Villa Devereux. The Economic Adviser must have winced in 1978 when, after Hickman acquired a house which gave him the right of residence under Jersey's immigration law, he razed it to the ground. "Everything in this house results from irri-tation at conventionality," he proudly declares. "That's the wonder-ful thing about having money. You can make your fantasies come true."

Then there's Douglas and Dale Howe, emigrés from Hong Kong in search of a tax haven closer to Harrods and to their son's prep school. Jersey is thirty minutes from Heathrow: "The plane is just like a village bus, really." Mr Howe made a fortune out of writing a textbook on English as a foreign language while working for the British Council in Hong Kong. Mrs Howe is "having to learn to cook all over again, because we had to leave our Filipinos behind. Jersey people won't do anything like cleaning or gardening. Everyone has to import Portuguese."

Tax reliefs

Any tax relief or allowance is worth more than twice as much to top-rate taxpayers (those with incomes of at least £43,625 in 1987/88) as to the vast majority of people who only pay standard 27 per cent tax. Their effect is to reduce the amount of your income that gets taxed at the highest rate. So for someone who's got enough income to go into the 60 per cent bracket, a tax allowance of £1,000 for mortgage payments, say, pushes £1,000 less of their income into the 60 per cent bracket, saving £600. But if you only pay standard-rate tax, at 27 per cent, the amount you pay tax on goes down by £1,000, saving only £270. Instead of saying that you get a "tax allowance" of £1,000, the Inland Revenue should give you an "allowance against tax" of £270, which would be the same whatever your top rate of tax. This is what the Labour Party means when it talks of "restricting tax relief to the standard rate", and it's a shame the SDP is better at explaining it.

Mortgage tax relief appears the most "democratic" of tax subsidies, as it's used by nearly 40 per cent of the population.[6] But it is the target of almost universal criticism, some of it a little misplaced. The real unfairnesses in the tax treatment of homes are higher-rate relief, the Capital Gains Tax exemption and the fact that home owners don't have to pay rent. Mortgage tax relief itself will always survive, because there would be too many losers among the electorally marginal upper working class if it were replaced. The only system that could replace it would be a Politically Volatile Socio-Economic Group subsidy. The prospect of a return to Schedule A taxation — the days before 1963 when homeowners were taxed on the value of the rent they saved by owning their own home — is equally if not more remote.

Many tax reliefs and exemptions seem at first sight to be eminently reasonable, for example the fact that prizes and awards are tax free, until it's seen how they can operate in practice. It may seem all right to let a penniless author take home the £10,000 Booker Prize, but is it fair that the Duke of Devonshire should keep all the £136,922 he won with Park Top, a horse he bought for a mere five hundred guineas — £525 to you and me?

Some reliefs and exemptions make taxes so feeble that you might as well abolish them altogether. This is what happened to Capital Transfer Tax. Even in January 1985, "Capital Transfer Tax is now viewed like an infectious illness," advised Professor Anthony Mellows in *Harpers and Queen*. "One only suffers if one fails to take precautions." He predicted that Capital Transfer Tax rates were never likely to be so low again, and suggested that for the more wealthy

> there is much to be said for making substantial lifetime gifts and accepting that tax will become payable. The reductions in the rates of Capital Transfer Tax which this government has made, particularly in the last Budget, mean that the rate of tax on lifetime gifts, however large in value, can never exceed 30 per cent.

Mellows, who made money (but presumably not much) before the 1983 election selling advice on how to get your money out of the country before a Labour government brought exchange controls back, advised that future "adjustments" in Capital Transfer Tax rates were more likely to be up than down. How he underestimated the Conservative government's devotion to "family property"! As the late Liberal MP David Penhaligon commented in the 1986 Budget debate,

> I rather suspect that a fair amount of capital has been transferred in the past few years in the belief that the regime could not conceivably become more favourable. It just shows what mistakes people can make. If only they had hung on a bit longer, they would have paid no tax at all.

In his 1986 Budget, Nigel Lawson abolished lifetime Capital Transfer Tax and allowed people to avoid the new Inheritance Tax altogether if they passed their wealth on more than seven years before death. It's difficult to know from the official record what the parliamentary debate on the Budget was really like, but Labour MP Dale Campbell-Savours gives a good impression of someone deranged with frustration and anger. He begged the government: "Please stop it." He was ordered by the Speaker to withdraw the remark "I bet that the honourable member for Dorset North [Tory MP Nicholas Baker] is a beneficiary. He shakes his pocket in shame." Then he demanded that the sitting be suspended until a Treasury minister could provide a figure for the amount of tax lost through changes to Capital Transfer Tax since 1979.

It looked as if the Chancellor was replacing a fairly feeble tax on all capital transfers with a completely avoidable tax on transfers at death. Not only can you take out an insurance policy against dying early, but if you die between three and seven years after handing over your assets you only pay between four-fifths and one-fifth of the full tax.

Peter Wyman, partner in accountants Deloittes, thought this was as low as the Chancellor would go:

As the general election looms in the not too distant future, it is wise to regard the absence of tax on lifetime gifts as a measure which might last only for the next twelve months, so people who may benefit from this relaxation should take their courage in their hands and set about obtaining professional advice (*Accountancy Age* Magazine, May 1986).

Let us praise the courage of the super-rich. "Once the Finance Bill is enacted the brave will be able to make arrangements which will secure the future of their family business for one or even two further generations."

Wyman was a bit upset, though, about one aspect of the measure. "It is a great shame that the discretionary trust, that most versatile of vehicles, has been hammered yet again," he says. A vehicle, that is, for the noble purpose of preserving the hard-earned money of the rich from contributing to the vulgar business of the common weal, and the equally noble purpose of employing deserving tax accountants like Mr Wyman.

He was not half as upset as some of the rich against whom Dale Campbell-Savours railed so passionately. The Duke of Devonshire's solicitors, Currey and Co, wrote to the *Financial Times* to protest, in effect, that the Duke had stashed all the family wealth in trusts, which the Chancellor proposed to go on taxing exactly as before, under the old Capital Transfer Tax rules. Any transfers into or out of trusts would be taxed at the old rates, during the donor's life or on death. An ungrateful lot, but the Duke had a point. Overall, the burden of Inheritance Tax is much lighter than Capital Transfer Tax, but the burden was lifted in a selective way. The old rich, with family money tied up in trusts, and the middling sort of Tory supporter, most of whose wealth is tied up in the house, did least well out of the change, and indeed some accountants believe some people will pay more tax as a result.

The Chancellor's argument for abolishing the tax on lifetime transfers was that it would improve the incentive for small business owners to develop their business and hand it on to their heirs. "By deterring lifetime giving, [Capital Transfer Tax] has had the effect of locking in assets, particularly the ownership of family businesses, often to the detriment of the businesses concerned," he said in his Budget speech. He was backed up by other Tories, although not by any evidence. Michael Heseltine, returned to the back benches after the Westland affair, said the change was "an important part of maintaining the capitalist strength of Britain", and he and other MPs complained about Capital Transfer Tax forcing family businesses to sell out, "with the consequent loss of jobs".

Desperate excuses for his boss's propaganda drive were wearing a bit thin when junior Treasury minister Peter Brooke added: "Some businesses go wrong because entrepreneurs stay in control of a business too long, which is sometimes because the tax structure prevents them from handing over the responsibility for the business earlier." Social Democrat Ian Wrigglesworth MP pointed out that the owners of businesses already got half or a third off their Capital Transfer Tax bill through special reliefs. This was estimated to cost the Exchequer £20 million in 1983/84, which means that small businesses accounted for a mere 5 per cent of assets liable to Capital Transfer Tax. If the tax really were a damaging burden on small business, which it isn't, the solution would be to exempt small businesses altogether, not the 95 per cent of non-business assets.

So why did he do it? Was it a misjudged bid to appease the party faithful? The idea of the state interfering in family "gifts" has always been distasteful to the Conservatives, although the Macmillan wing of the party would have accepted it as a way of forcing the vulgar rich to accept their "responsibility" to society as a whole.

The abolition of Capital Transfer Tax in the 1986 Budget was partly symbolic, being of cultural significance in asserting the soaring social value being placed on "family money". The Conservatives had already drawn the teeth of Capital Transfer Tax. Even in 1979, when its dismantling began, it only had dentures and a rather weak jaw, for when Denis Healey created it in 1975, he departed from his "squeezing the rich until the pips squeak" prospectus by taxing lifetime transfers at a lower rate and allowing reliefs for farms, small businesses and anything else rich people might own.

Nigel Lawson's 1986 Budget was the boldest statement of the covert principle of all previous Thatcher budgets: wealth shall not be taxed. It completes the silent revolution of the British tax system — the removal of taxes on capital. Once you've got it, it's effectively outside the tax system, and with a bit of planning can accumulate and be passed on in the tax-free stratosphere below which we lesser mortals labour. This principle was concealed at first because Geoffrey Howe's début Budget in 1979 dramatically cut *income* tax rates for those on high incomes, and compensated by doubling VAT. But it has been adopted as official policy, albeit in a discreet paragraph of a faceless Treasury document:

> The Government believe that there is no case whatsoever for maintaining a system of capital taxes which, by holding back business success and penalising personal endeavour, does economic and social damage ("The 1982 Budget: the Strategy", *Economic Progress Report* No 143, March 1982).

Sophistic textual analysis might suggest that the government's distaste is limited only to those capital taxes which allegedly hold back and penalise — indeed Geoffrey Howe has accepted the case in principle for some capital taxes: "There is, of course, a place for capital taxation, including in particular a charge on death. But change is needed" (1980 Budget speech).

The Treasury statement would be quite consistent with the government's hostility to domestic rates — it is by instinct and ideology against any taxes on capital whatsoever — on the existence, accumulation or transfer of wealth. It continues with them only because they still bring in as much money as a small privatisation.

Tax Reform

Tax reformers resemble computer fantasy game-players, American football enthusiasts or local election statisticians. Each one has a pet scheme — usually not very well house-trained — intended to simplify the present rambling structure and make it fairer and easier to understand. Often, this involves an entirely new set of jargon tacked on to elements of the existing system that means nothing to people's everyday lives: integration of NICs, graduated rates scheme, expenditure tax, negative income tax.

One of the few groups able to popularise the cause of tax reform is the Institute for Fiscal Studies. This is not good for the Left. Although it was set up by Social Democrats, and the quality of its research and analysis is very high, the IFS has handed the Conservatives three gifts on a plate: by lending its credibility to the idea of fiscal neutrality, to the notion that the present tax system is especially progressive (meaning it takes proportionately more from the rich) and to proposals for an "expenditure tax".

Fiscal neutrality is the doctrine that taxes shouldn't distort economic decisions, and shouldn't discriminate between different forms of economic activity. This fits snugly with the Tory notion of freedom defined as freedom from state interference in economic activity — particularly the accumulation and enjoyment of wealth. The idea that taxes shouldn't influence economic decisions is a powerful argument against taxing the rich more than the poor, and indeed against any form of taxation.

The whole point about a progressive tax system is that it should take *proportionately* more from those more able to pay, that is, that it *should* discriminate — against the rich and in favour of the poor.

Progressive and redistributive taxation

"The tax system is now more progressive than at any time since the post-war period," said John Kay, then director of the Institute for Fiscal Studies, after the 1985 Budget. The usual definition of a "progressive" tax is that given by John Kay and Mervyn King in *The British Tax System* (second edition): a tax is progressive "if the rich pay relatively more than the poor". This only raises the question: relative to what? In later editions, they change their definition, and emphasise the effect of all taxes taken together.

Income tax is usually considered to be progressive if the proportion of income paid in tax rises relative to income. On the whole, it does. Even if you only pay standard 27 per cent income tax, the proportion of your whole income that goes in income tax rises when your income does — if you earn less than the personal allowance you pay 0 per cent; if you earn twice as much as the personal allowance you pay 13.5 per cent of your total income in tax, and so on.

However, National Insurance contributions are also a tax on income, and are often not taken into account when discussing income tax. Most full-time employees — that is, those in a company pension scheme — pay 6.85 per cent, making the "standard" tax-on-income rate 33.85 per cent. For people who aren't in a company pension scheme (who are in the State Earnings-Related Pension Scheme, SERPS), National Insurance is 9 per cent, making the standard rate of tax on income 36 per cent.

What's more, you don't pay any extra contributions if you earn over £15,340 a year (1986/87). So between £15,340 and the next income-tax band, the combined tax rate on each extra pound earned drops back to 27 per cent again. Income tax goes up to 40 per cent above £20,325 for single people without mortgages or other allowances, or £21,695 for couples. At £26,870 it pays for a married couple to "elect" to be taxed separately (if the wife is earning more than £6,545), and to go back down to 27 per cent once more, although this time it's partly offset by the loss of the Married Man's Allowance.

The proportion of total income taken by income tax and National Insurance together drops from 29.9 per cent to 29.2 per cent, for a single person with no other allowances between the income of £15,340 and £20,325. That is rather less "progressive" than is usually made out. Indeed, John Kay's colleagues at the Institute for Fiscal Studies, Nick Morris and Ian Preston, concluded their detailed analysis of the actual effects of taxes and benefits between 1968 and 1983 by saying: "The tax system became less good at redistribution." [7]

The income-tax rate then rises in 5 per cent steps to 60 per cent. Again, 60 per cent is the "headline" figure (known as the *marginal* rate, because each additional or "marginal" £1 earned is taxed at 60 per cent). There are two reasons why the 60 per cent figure is misleading. Even if anyone paid tax at that rate, the total tax bill for someone on a salary of about £50,000 (the point at which the 60 per cent rate would begin if it weren't for various allowances) would be about 48 per cent including National Insurance. But very few people pay an effective marginal tax rate of 60 per cent because of pension contribution relief. People under fifty-three can pay 17.5 per cent of their income into their pension fund free of tax, and so pay tax on 60 per cent of the remaining 82.5 per cent, which is really a rate of 49.5 per cent. [8] The 17.5 per cent is "deferred income" which, when taken in the form of a pension, might eventually be taxed at, say, the standard rate, but until then it accumulates and earns interest entirely free of tax, which more than covers any eventual tax bill.

Indeed, it is perfectly possible for someone on a salary of £100,000 a year to pay £13,150 tax in 1987/88, a total of 13 per cent (using the Married Man's Allowance, full mortgage and pension relief and making a £40,000 a year investment under the Business Expansion Scheme), and for a self-employed person no tax at all.

Once into the stratosphere, the rich often find that the increase in their wealth is no longer called "income" anyway, but is called "capital gain" and is taxed at 30 per cent (after allowing for inflation and a big exempt amount, currently £6,600 a year). Nothing "progressive" about that distinction. Capital Gains Tax raises less than 1 per cent of total tax revenue. VAT and local rates, on the other hand, together produce almost as much as taxes on income. VAT is generally regressive, but slightly progressive at the lower end of the scale, because things that form a larger part of the poor's budget (like food, housing, gas, electricity and children's clothing) are exempt. However, inflation in the prices of these same VAT-exempt essentials has been higher than average since 1979,[9] in the case of gas and electricity because of deliberate government policy towards nationalised industries that amounts to backdoor taxation.

The only significant tax that is intended to be levied on wealth is rates. No wonder Mrs Thatcher wants to abolish it: not because it falls more heavily on the rich than the poor — it doesn't — but on principle, because rates are the closest thing in Britain to a wealth tax. Partly because rates are levied on notional values that haven't been reassessed since 1973, they are in practice regressive, although they have a slight progressive kink at the bottom because of housing benefit (what used to be rent and rate rebates).

How progressive a tax is should really be measured against the tax-payer's overall "taxable capacity", which should incorporate both income and wealth. The theory of taxes in Britain has always been that they should be paid out of income, except on death (even rates are notionally a levy on the rental value of property). But "from each according to their means" must include wealth. That's why Chapter 7 defined "rich" in terms of income plus notional income from wealth; and why a genuinely progressive tax system should tax capital gain the same as interest, dividends or rent from wealth. This way, any additions to wealth are taxed progressively. To be *redistributive*, however, more income or wealth has to be allocated to the poor, and/or a direct levy on wealth (even just a one-off) has to be imposed. The tax-benefit system continues to be progressive under the Conservatives, but it has ceased to be redistributive, in that the rich are getting richer faster than tax is taking away from them, and benefits are not going up fast enough to enable the poor to keep up.

An "expenditure tax"

Another of the Institute for Fiscal Studies' *bête blanches*, an expenditure tax is a way of taxing people on their standard of living and encouraging them to save, while eliminating the favoured status of certain kinds of saving, such as pensions. It involves paying tax on income you spend and not income you save: any money you put into officially recognised forms of saving is deducted from your income before calculating tax. When you take money out of your savings, it is added to your income for tax purposes.

An expenditure tax was first given credence by the Meade Report on tax reform in 1978, commissioned by the last Labour government. The Institute for Fiscal Studies has been preaching of the gospel ever since, lending its credibility to an idea which is unfortunately irrelevant to genuine tax reform. In 1985, the Social Democratic Party and the Confederation of British Industry both adopted the proposal, "as a basis for discussion", within weeks of each other. The CBI's discussion paper, *Tax: Time for Change* (December 1985), is particularly hypocritical, seizing on "fiscal neutrality" and arguing against "special pleading" before going on to propose the abolition of all taxes on business!

An expenditure tax is a proper intellectual solution to the problems of ad hoc and contradictory taxes. But mention of it causes 90 per cent of the population instantly to switch off and the other 10 per cent to think you're talking about VAT. It is a wonderful weapon for conservatives masquerading as tax reformers.

But the real drawback of an expenditure tax is that to introduce it, many more anomalies and complexities have to be created for several years — when one of the main purposes of such a system would be to make the tax system simpler and more coherent. It is not a system to adopt if we are starting from here. It cannot be introduced overnight because the sudden exemption of various forms of saving would cut tax revenue dramatically — almost exclusively to the benefit of the rich. The CBI proposes phasing it in by tenths over a decade, while the SDP wants to exempt various forms of savings piecemeal over a transitional period.

It would be far better to start with the system we've got, much of which *is* well understood, and extend it towards widely-supported political aims: greater equality, taxation according to ability to pay and fairness as between earnings from work and the profits of ownership.

The idiot's guide to better taxes looks something like this:

- high tax rates are pointless; the 98 per cent top rate on unearned income under the last Labour government brought in very little money and undermined socialist images of generosity and mutual support. It's much better to make sure there are fewer ways round the tax rates you've got; hence
- the same progressive rates, taking National Insurance into account, should apply to income both from employment and

investments, including income in the form of capital gain;

- tax reliefs, exemptions and allowances — where they can't be got rid of — shouldn't benefit the rich more than the poor; and
- the use of trusts, companies and abroad to avoid tax should be reduced.

The first three points are matters of detailed policy, the precise design of which depends on the political circumstances at the time. The Labour Party's plans for tax changes are patchy, but broadly follow this prospectus.

The fourth point, however, the problems of trusts, companies and tax havens, is not something politicians of any of the opposition parties have given much thought to. As long as British law allows for legal entities other than persons, trusts and companies will go on being used. If you can put money into a company or a trust, or transfer it abroad, instead of receiving it as an individual and paying tax on it, you can postpone paying tax and earn interest on it meanwhile, or avoid paying tax altogether.

Of course, you can't get away with it that easily. Discretionary trusts are supposed to pay income tax at 45 per cent on their income, plus a 9 per cent capital levy every ten years; "close" companies (broadly, ones that are family-controlled) have to pay tax on profits as if they were the income of the shareholders; money paid to British residents from offshore trusts or companies has in theory to be taxed as income, capital gain or transfer as appropriate. But in practice there are unobtrusive gaps big enough to drive the family Bentley through.

It's a little harder to abolish the existence of other countries in the world — and not necessarily a desirable project. The principle that all British taxes due must be paid when sums of money or assets leave the country again has holes in it in practice — such as the deferral of Capital Gains Tax until gains are "realised". The act of transferring money across national borders ought to be a taxable event. For example, if someone owns a business through an offshore trust, and the trust sells some shares, any capital gain should be taxed "on exit", as if it were going to an individual. Likewise, anything coming into the country to an individual, trust or family company should be taxed as income unless the taxpayer can show that it already has been.

One of the simpler reforms would be to end the tax haven status of the Channel Islands and the Isle of Man, and to discourage the use of British dependencies like the Cayman Islands and the Turks and Caicos for tax avoidance.

Taxing Inheritance

The really difficult question, however, is what to do about taxing the transfer of wealth from one generation to the next. Here we get to where what is politically possible begins to diverge from what the Labour Party believes is politically possible. (The Labour Party is also timid about Capital Gains Tax, insisting on keeping a threshold before capital gains become taxable despite the fact that this is an allowance which favours those who already have. Poor people simply do not hold assets that show capital gains. They have building society or Trustee Savings Bank accounts and pay tax on the interest, deducted at source.)

The fairest and most logical method would be to tax inherited wealth (or wealth passed on during a lifetime) as the income of the recipient. This is likely to be unpopular, introducing a tax charge on the most modest of bequests and inducing apoplexy among the rich. The ideological roots of the desire to pass on wealth — in the form of "providing for one's dependants" — are very deep. It means that universal state provision isn't enough to guarantee popular support for the abolition of inheritance. As Geoffrey Howe so percipiently remarked before the invention of Thatcherism: "Clearly, if you start with a society founded on families, there are bound to be inequalities." ("Whatever Happened to Equality?", BBC Radio 3 series, 1973/74.) The family is at the root of inequality. It is inherently inegalitarian, and, through its interaction with ethnicity, patriarchy and class (especially through education), powerfully reactionary.

The problem is that the emotional attraction of providing after one's death for self-selected good causes is not intrinsically an unsocialist desire. But the desire to provide for one's dependants and family is a useful one to the ruling class and its dynasts. Merchant bank Hill Samuel's tax advice advertisements claimed (before the abolition of Capital Transfer Tax in 1986): "They can't tax you when you die, so they tax your children instead."

Ideologically, the focal point of the struggle is over primogeniture. It is the retention of family wealth in a dynastic block, over which the eldest male exercises temporary stewardship, that gels the existing concentration of wealth. What is wrong with Mrs

Thatcher's "cascade of wealth down the family line" is its linearity: family wealth should be encouraged to cascade in a widening delta.

If the principle of really heavy taxation of inherited wealth can't initially win a popular mandate, the principle of taxing it according to the amount received would at least help to disperse concentrations of wealth, not just beyond the sole heir, but also beyond the nuclear family of spouse and children.

What About a Wealth Tax?

Ever since 1972, the Labour Party has been committed to bringing in a direct tax on wealth. It was actively considered in the 1960s (see p. 144), but it was actually promised in the 1974 manifesto, and Chancellor Denis Healey predicted at the Blackpool conference that year that there would be "howls of anguish" from the rich, although not necessarily about the wealth tax. According to Adrian Ham, economic assistant to Healey until the IMF crisis in 1976, Treasury officials thought a wealth tax was "perfectly feasible", but it was killed "on instructions from Downing Street". Harold Wilson didn't want the legislative complications of bringing the tax in, and "there was no groundswell of support for it, no group was pressing for it".

Labour's commitment to an annual wealth tax hasn't been updated since *Labour's Programme 1982*, when it was intended to tax the richest "1 per cent or so" of the population, with the exemption limit set at around £150,000 per individual adult in 1982 prices (worth £180,000 in 1986). Homes and pension rights would not be exempt (although only a tiny minority of these would be taxable). The tax rate was not specified, but the tax was expected to raise up to £1,000 million (updated to 1986 prices), which implies a rate of around 1 per cent (on the amount above the exemption limit only).

If public support for taxing the dead is uncertain, what hope is there for Labour winning a popular mandate for a wealth tax on the living? Quite a lot, actually. The Gallup poll (February 1986) for London Weekend Television's *Fortune* found that a wealth tax may not be a total vote-loser: 42 per cent supported a wealth tax, with 45 per cent against and 13 per cent undecided. However, that may prove to be the high point of popularity once the propagandists of the rich launch their campaign.

The Irish experience of a wealth tax (1975–78) poses much more serious practical obstacles. It suggests that it will raise much less money than expected, be easily the most expensive tax to administer

— and could be a political disaster. In Ireland, an average of 2,400 people paid the tax in each of its three years of life, raising a miserable £5 million a year. Yet it was a major political issue for several years and one which the Fine Gael party believed damaged it considerably.

Reflecting on the lessons of the Irish wealth tax debacle for British parties, Professor Cedric Sandford and Oliver Morrissey write that neither the Labour nor the Conservative parties

> has anything like the research backing which, or example, underpins the major West German political parties. In the UK much of the input comes from voluntary advisers. Whereas on tax matters the UK Labour Party has never lacked advice from macroeconomists, it has been thin on the practical input from advisers with an administrative, accountancy and business background, where the Conservatives have been strong (*The Irish Wealth Tax*).

However, there is a very strong argument in favour of a wealth tax. It is that taxes on the transfer of capital take time to distribute wealth more equally. The Tories weakened Capital Transfer Tax after only four years, before it could have any real effect; their abolition of CTT on lifetime transfers in 1986 means that another generation of wealth transmission has been lost to tax. Equalising wealth through taxes on transfers is a process beyond the scope of a single parliament, and so Labour ought to have a policy for a short, sharp shock to move towards that goal through a levy such as a wealth tax.

But it's probably better not to have a wealth tax than to have one which vested interests had half-eaten in parliamentary committee. It would then be unfair and a great deal of time, money and effort would be put into avoiding it. As with taxing inheritance it can confidently be predicted that a Labour government would have great difficulty fighting off the business lobby. Business people will argue that they will be forced to sell up or break up the business to pay taxes on the wealth represented by the company. This argument has more force with a wealth tax. For death duties the argument implies that the taxpayer's heir has some government-given right to run a wholly-owned business as her or his parent did — or that selling the business is impossible or a bad thing. To pay a wealth tax a part-share of the business may have to be sold, which can be difficult, although it could be dealt with by involving enterprise boards in taking stakes in local businesses in lieu of tax.

Meanwhile, what scope is there for developing the tax on wealth we already have? Rates are a tax on property, which is the largest element of personal wealth in this country. They could be made easier to understand and the burden shifted to richer property-owners if they were levied on the capital value of property, instead of the obscure concept of "imputed rent" as it was in 1973 (the Conservatives avoided the revaluation due in 1983, which would have made the burden fairer but would have produced the sort of outcry the 1985 Scottish revaluation provoked — only worse). Rates have a lot wrong with them, but they are a crude form of wealth tax, and a threshold and/or higher rates of rates (that is, "poundage") on more expensive properties could relieve the burden on the poor.

A substitute for a full wealth tax could be to levy a national "super rate" on all domestic property above a certain value. The tax could be deferred and paid on death to avoid newspaper stories of widows forced to sell up to pay their super-rate bills. But it would be simpler to administer and harder to avoid or evade than a wealth tax. If the rich don't emigrate, they've got to live somewhere. But if you really want to clobber the richest 1 per cent selectively, a wealth tax is the only way, because most of their wealth is in stocks and shares and business assets.

---

1. See, for example, the figures given by Michael Stewart, an adviser and generally a supporter of the 1964–70 government, in *The Labour Government's Economic Record 1964*–70 (see Bibliography on p. 185). Central Statistical Office figures (in *Social Trends 1980*, HMSO) show a similar picture, comparing state pensions and Supplementary Benefit (or National Assistance) with personal disposable income per head (the level of Supplementary Benefit rose from about 55 per cent of disposable income per head in 1964 to nearly 59 per cent in 1970, but in 1965 had been nearly 62 per cent).

2. Inland Revenue, *Report*, 1985.

3. Civil and Public Services Association newspaper *Red Tape*, August (2) 1986, outline of joint claim with the Society of Civil and Public Servants for 1,700 jobs.

4. "International Comparisons of Taxes and Social Security Contributions in 20 OECD countries 1973–83", *Economic Trends*, May 1986. Taxes, including rates and National Insurance contributions, as a proportion of gross national product rose from 38 per cent in UK in 1978 to 44 per cent in 1983, while the UK remained tenth out of the twenty countries. In 1983 Sweden had the highest taxes, at 59 per cent, France (51 per cent), Italy (47 per cent) and West Germany (46 per cent) came above the UK. Japan (30 per cent) came bottom, just below the United States (31 per cent).

5. *Stevenson v Wishart*, 1985.

6. Estimate based on the calculation, on p. 61, of proportion of adult population who are home owners. Two-thirds of owner-occupied homes are owned with a mortgage.

7. "Taxes, benefits and the distribution of income 1968–83", *Fiscal Studies*, Institute for Fiscal Studies, November 1986. Their analysis showed that in 1983 the tax system was regressive for the bottom 25 per cent of the population (that is, they paid a greater proportion of their market income — before benefits — in taxes than those above them).

8. People aged over fifty-three can make even bigger tax-free contributions to their pension, of up to 25.6 per cent.

9. Fry and Pashardes, *Fiscal Studies*, Institute for Fiscal Studies, Winter 1985. The poor have suffered from differential inflation rates since before 1979, *Low Pay Review*, 23, Low Pay Unit, November 1985.

11. CONCLUSION

"I do not condone or excuse the poverty and insecurity in the basic necessities of life which we have today as a legacy of unrestrained competition and uneconomic waste and redundancy. We have to evolve a new system by which the supply of those articles which we have classified as being of common need would be absorbed into an amplified conception of the social services." — Harold Macmillan *The Middle Way*, 1938.

Some readers may be puzzled that Part II of this book dwells so much on the difficulties of sharing out income and wealth more equally. The rich have got richer and the poor have got poorer, they might say, which is wrong, and so the rich ought to have it taken away from them. But why has this urgent moral imperative been frustrated in the past and effectively marginalised in the past eight years?

People *do* want greater equality. But "steal from the rich to give the poor" is not enough as a programme for government. While people may will the end, they often find they are not keen on the means, or that politicians decide on their behalf that they wouldn't be if they knew what was involved. How can egalitarians devise a programme which both redistributes from rich to poor in the short term and mobilises public opinion behind continuing change?

It may not be precisely phrased, but it is overwhelmingly understood by the British people that under the Conservatives "the rich get richer, the poor get poorer". Asked by Gallup in November 1979, 71 per cent agreed and 18 per cent disagreed.[1] The question was then repeated each March:

	1981	1983	1985
Agree	70	74	79
Disagree	20	17	13

That this is wrong is less overwhelmingly believed to be the case by the electorate (witness the fact that three months after the March 1983 finding the Conservatives were returned to office). But the British do not approve of the rich and poor going their separate ways. In December 1985, 60 per cent agreed that "income and wealth should be redistributed towards ordinary working people", and only 24 per cent disagreed. And there was a huge majority in favour of extending "government services such as health, education and welfare, even if it means some increases in taxes" (59 per cent in favour, 16 per cent for tax cuts even if services are cut, 18 per cent for the status quo — a big change over the Thatcher years: in March 1979 there was an even split).

But support for redistribution is fairly shallow. Although 41 per cent of people in the 1985 British Social Attitudes Survey agreed that "income and wealth should be redistributed towards ordinary working people" (28 per cent disagreed, 29 per cent offered no opinion), only 14 per cent of the population "agreed strongly". [2]

More detailed polling carried out by Gallup in February 1986 for LWT's *Fortune* programme shows up attitudes more clearly. While 70 per cent agreed with the mild judgement that the "gap between rich and poor is too big", and 58 per cent favoured "redistributing from rich to poor", only 35 per cent felt strongly enough to agree that it was actually "unjust" that some people were much richer than others.

All the same, very large numbers of people are prepared to support measures so "radical" that they are not even on the contemporary political agenda: 42 per cent favoured a wealth tax and 33 per cent a "limit of individual wealth". Curiously, while older people (over forty-five) were *less* likely to think the gap between rich and poor was too big, or to want in general terms to redistribute from the one to the other, they were *more* likely to support the specific measures of a wealth tax or an individual maximum. In the over sixty-five age group *more* people (53 per cent) were in favour of a wealth tax than in favour of the general "redistribution" proposition (51 per cent). So it seems that young people have a greater idealistic desire for more equality which tends to collapse to lower levels of support for specific measures to bring it about. Older people, perhaps more cynical or simply having thought about it more, are less likely to believe in redistribution, but those who do believe in it have a firmer belief than the young, backed by a willingness to see stringent measures brought in.

The propagandists of the rich have always found ways to soften political demands for greater equality, and their advisers have always found ways to get round the taxes that softened politicians have enacted. But if a reforming government knew what it was about, surely it could succeed by skill rather than bludgeon?

The purpose of Part II of this book is to examine the weak points in the structures — ideological and economic — which sustain inequality. We start with the moral strength of egalitarianism, but have to work round the opposing strength of the Right's appeal to "family" and "liberty". The mobilising force of an egalitarian programme ought to be the perception of a minimum decent standard of living. This is to do with "levelling up" rather than levelling down, and any sacrifices that have to be made are directly linked to the elimination of poverty.

Chapter 7 provided a definition of those who have no "moral" right to be as rich as they are. A 100 per cent tax rate would be *morally* justified on income above this level, but if the top rate were left at 60 per cent a large part of the Right's propaganda would implode, while wholesale scrapping of tax reliefs could be much more effective in taking more in income tax from the rich.[3] The definition does not absolve others of those who are not poor of moral responsibility to bear a share of the costs of eliminating poverty; but it is urgent that the Labour Party doesn't allow itself to be portrayed as the Higher Taxes Party — especially in the light of the Tory record (see p. 149). So it is worth attacking poverty more slowly than would otherwise be the case in order to reduce the tax burden on and a little way above average earnings, and to target increased taxation as much as possible on those defined in Chapter 7 as rich.

The tax, benefit and state pensions régime is the most important way of expressing and enforcing democratic aspirations as to how a nation's resources should be allocated. But it is essentially about modifying the allocation of resources by "the market" after the event, rather than modifying the way the market itself operates.

Changing the *conditions* in which markets work will have the most dramatic short-term effect. Some urgent equalising measures are taken for granted of a non-Tory government: more jobs, better pensions, benefits, health and education services. But the *rules* under which markets work must also be changed to bring about longer-term redistribution of incomes. Measures such as a National Minimum Wage and equal pay for work of equal value (including part-time work), especially if enforced by making public-sector purchasing conditional on them ("contract compliance"), would start to have an effect straight away but would take time to build up. They need to be accompanied by measures to break up the restrictions which help bid up the pay of professional and managerial groups.

In turn, this means undermining concentrations of private wealth and power. Is the future of egalitarianism to be "upon the basis of the common ownership of the means of production, distribution and exchange"?[4] Or is it to be upon the basis of the mixed economy, with the mix consisting of rather more of the private sector than before 1979? Or is there something in between, a newer style of socialism which recognises the greater individualism of the age, and the many inequalities which overlie class differences?

"Equality" is not a simple, single concept. The reasons why some people are materially better off than others in Britain in the 1980s criss-cross and reinforce each other, building an edifice of inequality that is difficult to break down in an even-handed way. Positive discrimination in favour of women, ethnic minorities, disabled people or comprehensive school pupils offends a meritocratic concept of "fairness". Prohibiting private education appears to threaten the liberties of the few far more seriously than permitting it appears to threaten the liberties of the many. Tax rates of 100 per cent seem to nullify creative economic activity without providing the inspiration to an alternative.

But support for the redistribution of power can be mobilised through the use of positive images in the language of democracy, as the Greater London Council showed before it was abolished by the Conservative government in 1986. Ballots could be extended from trade unions to companies, not just on political donations but on takeovers and some management appointments. Comprehensive education has to be promoted in terms of the same choice and opportunity for all, so that any parents who want to send their children to Eton should be allowed to do so whether or not they pay.

What is to be done in the meantime about the existing unequal distribution of wealth? Comparing the British situation with that of other countries (or those with which comparisons can be made, see p. 16) demonstrates how durable the structures of inequality are. The degree of wealth inequality in Britain today is similar in other democratic industrialised countries, and may represent a norm towards which European countries moved during the middle two quarters of the 20th century, and at which the countries of the Old Commonwealth and the US already were, with their different colonial/settler history. On the other hand, the notion that the present level of inequality is immutable is plainly absurd.

The key problem is inheritance. As Josiah Wedgwood, the

philanthropic Liberal MP, pointed out in 1929: "The ethical arguments in favour of claims to inherit are extraordinarily weak" (*The Economics of Inheritance*). However weak, they have yet to be defeated, but the *Fortune* opinion poll finding — that 33 per cent want to see an absolute limit to the amount of wealth an individual may own — suggests that public support could at least be won for an upper limit to the amount any one individual can inherit.

In practice "taking it away from them" is likely to be a slow process, and so is the building up of compensating wealth for the dispossessed. The significance of the Swedish "workers' funds" set up in 1984 is that they are an attempt to build up the quantities of wealth and power under "common ownership" in a mixed economy. The funds are being built up out of a profits tax on business, and are being invested by regional boards controlled by trade unionists. They have been bitterly resisted by business interests, and their objectives are confused, but they are potentially the vehicle for genuine common ownership by employees. The opposition they've aroused can be explained by comparing them with pension funds, which are not genuinely owned collectively and which are safely managed by capitalists.[5]

Much faster progress could be made by democratising existing stores of wealth — not by "privatising" them to powerless and isolated individuals, but by, say, "capturing" Britain's pension funds for their individual owners collectively under democratic control, either through trade unions or directly through a new mechanism.

This is where Neil Kinnock's idea of the "enabling state" comes in: "We want to put the state where it belongs in a democracy: not over the heads of the people, but under the feet of the people." Nationalisation of big industries didn't succeed in taking economic power "for the people", and privatisation has now restored and reinforced the old inequalities. Mrs Thatcher has used the state to allow the concentration of wealth under the banner of free-market forces. The counter ideology is to use the state to promote a different sort of freedom, that of "free-people forces", by dispersing concentrations of wealth and power and guaranteeing freedom from poverty. "It isn't," as Neil Kinnock said at Bournemouth in 1985, "the state doing things instead of people who could do them better ... it is the state doing things that institutions — big corporate institutions, market institutions, rich, strong people — have not done and will not do with anything like the speed or on anything like the scale that is needed to handle change with consent."

1. Gordon Heald and Robert J. Wybrow, *The Gallup Survey of Britain*, Croom Helm 1986, p. 124.

2. Self-completion questionnaire filled in by 85 per cent of 1,804 interviewees, *British Social Attitudes: the 1986 report* (SCPR 1986). This survey also shows 45 per cent thinking it "definitely should be the government's responsibility to reduce income differences between rich and poor" (a further 24 per cent thought it "probably" should be the government's responsibility): either people think this "definitely" but not "strongly", or they are markedly less keen on *wealth* redistribution.

3. The effective top rate would of course be nearer 70 per cent under any non-Tory government, because it would extend National Insurance contributions (currently another 6.85 per cent) to all earnings, no matter how high.

4. Labour Party Constitution, Clause 4 part 4.

5. Paradoxically, one of the effects of the Swedish wage earner funds has been to give the Stockholm stock exchange a boost, benefiting the rich. But in the longer term, the Swedish trade union movement intends to use the funds' blocs of shares much more purposively than, for example, British pension fund managers. (Iraj Hashi and Athar Hussain, "The Employee Investment Funds in Sweden", *National Westminster Bank Quarterly Review*, May 1986; Martin Linton, *The Swedish Example*, Fabian pamphlet, 1985.)

APPENDIX: HOW RICH IS RICH?

TABLE 9

How Rich Are You?

Income, 1987
Earnings
Of full-time employees (38% of adults)

10% earn more than	£16,470
25% earn more than	£12,420
50% earn more than	£9,150
25% earn less than	£6,700
10% earn less than	£5,200

Of which, of the men (26% of adults)

0.05% earn more than	£88,000
0.5% earn more than	£45,000
2.5% earn more than	£27,500
10% earn more than	£18,060
25% earn more than	£13,650
50% earn more than	£10,310
25% earn less than	£7,870
10% earn less than	£6,140

Of the women (12% of adults)

0.01% earn more than	£36,000
0.75% earn more than	£22,000
4% earn more than	£15,400
10% earn more than	£12,080
25% earn more than	£9,250
50% earn more than	£6,870
25% earn less than	£5,400
10% earn less than	£4,430

Total income
(Include pensions, income from investments and property, and profits.)
Of married couples (61% of adults)
1.2% have joint incomes over   £42,000

4% have joint incomes over	£28,000
10% have joint incomes over	£21,000
20% have joint incomes over	£17,000
33% have joint incomes over	£14,000
50% have joint incomes over	£11,000

Of single people (39% of adults)

1% have incomes over	£21,000
2% have incomes over	£17,000
3.5% have incomes over	£14,000
7% have incomes over	£11,000
25% have incomes over	£6,700

Wealth, 1987

(If you own your home, deduct the amount of mortgage you still owe from your estimate of its value and divide by two if you own it jointly, add your financial assets and your best guess at the auction value of your possessions; ignore pension rights and life insurance.)

1% own more than	£208,000
2% own more than	£134,000
5% own more than	£81,000
10% own more than	£53,000
25% own more than	£26,000
50% own more than	£9,000

Sources

Earnings: New Earnings Surveys 1985 and 1986, each percentile projected to 1987 by the increase over 1985 (Department of Employment); percentiles above the top decile derived from Pareto-curve extrapolation of NES 1986 by Incomes Data Services (Top Pay Review 71, January 1987), plus 10 per cent.

All income: Survey of Personal Incomes 1982/83 (Inland Revenue), updated by average earnings to 1984 and then on the basis of New Earnings Surveys for the appropriate quantiles.

Wealth: Professor Tony Shorrocks's estimates of the 1986 wealth distribution, Inland Revenue (1986) estimates for 1984, revalued at 10 per cent a year, interpolated by log normal straight lines where necessary.

How rich is rich?

1. Using the "democratic" method based on the *Breadline Britain* survey of what most people think of as being too poor this book defines the rich as individuals with earnings of £15,200 *plus* wealth of £100,000 in 1986. The table on p. 100 shows the earnings and wealth values of the "rich" threshold at different levels of earnings for an individual, updated to 1987. The method used is outlined on p. 95: Those whose income, including notional income from their wealth, is greater than that level which, if all the income above it were transferred to the poor, would eliminate what most people think of as deprivation.

2. If we use the lower estimate of the numbers in poverty, the "rich line" moves up to income of £16,800 and wealth of £136,000 for an individual (see paragraphs 13 and 25).

The amount of money needed to get rid of poverty

3. The authors of the *Breadline Britain* survey estimate the amount of money needed to eradicate what most people think of as poverty (in the book, *Poor Britain*, based on the television series). They found that most poverty would end if Supplementary Benefit was increased by half and if housing were improved to a basic standard. (Repeat of health warning: this isn't a plan for actually going about getting rid of poverty. Any practical system of more progressive taxes and benefits would take money away from more people than just "the rich", and would improve the lot of many relatively poor people who aren't actually "in poverty".)

4. *Breadline Britain*'s central estimate of the number of adults in poverty (adjusted in proportion to population to include Northern Ireland by adding 2.9 per cent) in 1983 was 7.882 million. If they'd all been on Supplementary Benefit, the cost in 1983 of paying half as much benefit again would have been £6,834 million.

5. At the time there were actually 5.316 million adults claiming supplementary benefit or other means-tested state payments, so *Breadline Britain* suggests there were another 2.566 million adults who were "poor". Either they weren't claiming benefit, or the means test didn't recognise the things they lacked as making them poor. (This is consistent with official figures for families on "low incomes"; for example 8.8 million adults and children were on or below Supplementary Benefit level in 1983, and another 7.5 million were living on an income level between the Supplementary Benefit level and 40 per cent higher.)

Means tested benefits

Number (000s) of recipients in 1985/86 UK (Great Britain adjusted proportionally to include Northern Ireland)

Supplementary Pensions	1,760
Supplementary Benefit	2,794
Family Income Supplement	206
One Parent Benefit	556
Total	5,316

Source: *Social Trends 1986*

Not all the people that *Breadline Britain* suggests are in poverty need their income raised by 50 per cent (some, perhaps around 2 million in "less intense poverty", are between the Supplementary Benefit level and 150 per cent of it). But the authors of *Poor Britain* estimate that around one million adults would still be in poverty on 150 per cent of the Supplementary Benefit level. I have assumed that the two effects cancel each other out.

6. Then the *Breadline Britain* findings have to be updated to April 1986, the reference date for this definition of the rich (the update to the 1987 figures given on p. 100 is arrived at afterwards, by raising the earnings element of the threshold by 7.5 per cent and the wealth element by 10 per cent). The statistical division of the House of Commons library estimated that the numbers of those on or below the Supplementary Benefit level rose from 8.8 million in 1983 (the official DHSS figure) to 11.7 million. Applying the same multiple to the *Breadline Britain* estimate produces a figure for 1986 of 10.479 million. As the level of Supplementary Benefits has risen by up to 2 per cent, 10 million adults in poverty is taken as the starting point. The cost in 1986 (adjusting 1985/86 figures in line with the Retail Price Index) of paying 50 per cent more than average Supplementary Benefit to 10 million people would have been £9,769 million.

7. The cost of improving the housing of the poor to provide what are thought of as necessities can also be estimated. *Breadline Britain* found that an indoor loo, a bath and freedom from damp are regarded as necessities, and separate bedrooms for each child over 10 of different sex.

8. In 1981 there were 900,000 homes without a bath or indoor loo in England and Wales (*Social Trends 1986*). Figures are not available on damp. The Department of the Environment's 1985 *Enquiry into the Condition of Local Authority Housing Stock* estimated that the cost of "heating, insulation and works to remedy condensation", not all of which relates to damp, in the public sector in England was £4,028 million. It also estimated that "repairs to structure and external fabric", some of which must have related to damp, would cost £7,306 million. A total of £3,000 million (1985/86 prices) for eliminating serious damp in the public sector is a bare minimum.

9. As for the private sector, the government's Housing Condition Survey in 1981 found 1.2 million dwellings in England and Wales "unfit for human habitation", 900,000 of them in the private sector. This is a much-criticised and subjective description, but if it means anything, it must come within the *Breadline Britain* survey definition of unacceptable and hence a contributor to poverty.

> An unfit dwelling is one deemed to be so far defective in one or more of the following as not to be reasonably suitable for occupation: repair, stability, freedom from damp, internal arrangement, natural lighting, ventilation, water supply, drainage and sanitary conveniences, facilities for the preparation and cooking of food, and the disposal of waste water. (*Social Trends 1986*, part 8, Appendix)

Applying Shelter's estimate of current (1985/86) average cost per dwelling of remedying damp of £5,000 to this figure, on the basis that this would secure at least temporary relief from damp, leaks and cold, produces £4,500 million.

10. Installing baths or loos would cost around £500 per dwelling, given that building alterations or extensions are sometimes needed, adding up to £450 million. The cost of building new homes for the 80,000 homeless (England and Wales) in 1983 would be about £2,321 million in 1985/86 prices. (Based on Association of Metropolitan Authorities' estimate of £15,000 million as the cost of building 517,000 new homes, in July 1985.)

11. Altogether these housing costs come to £10,271 million for England and Wales, in 1985/86 prices. It's not possible to make a meaningful estimate of the cost of rehousing the 2 per cent of households (Great Britain, *General Household Survey 1983*) living in 1983 at a density of over one person per room, so this is very much a minimum. (Compare it with the AMA's estimate of the total bill of £73,500 million for complete renovation of the English housing stock and rehousing the homeless and overcrowded.) A percentage

grossing up for Scotland and Northern Ireland (+ 13.5 per cent), by population, gives £11,653 million. This is equivalent to £11,889 million in April 1986 prices (revalued by RPI). As we are working on the basis of annual income, we need to express this in terms of, say, the revenue local councils would need to provide these basic housing needs. If they borrowed at 10 per cent, this would be £1,189 million.

12. So the total annual amount of money that needed to be transferred to the poor to eliminate poverty, as democratically defined, in 1986 was £9,769 + £1,189 million = £11,156 million.

The modesty of the Labour Party's programme to fight poverty, currently costed at £3,500 million a year excluding housing costs, can be gauged from this calculation. This is not a criticism of that programme, however, as Labour's battered credibility could hardly sustain a higher figure in the short term.

13. The lower estimate of the numbers in poverty, based on the *Breadline Britain* figures excluding those who lack only one or two necessities, is 5.599 million. Updated in line with the House of Commons library estimate of the DHSS "low income" figures to 1986, this is 7.445 million. The "extra Supplementary Benefit cost" on this basis would be £7,273 million, so the annual total cost of eliminating poverty on this basis in 1986 was £8,609 million (including the same £1,189 million housing cost).

The "Rich Line"

14. To draw a rich line equivalent to the poverty line drawn by the *Breadline Britain* survey, we need to know the distribution of after-tax income, including imputed income from wealth, among the rich.

15. The fullest official information about the distribution of income at the top end of the income range is produced by the Inland Revenue, and therefore comes in the form of tax units, that is, men and their "dependants". (The distribution of income given in the *Survey of Personal Incomes* isn't complete, but the main omissions are state benefits and wages below the tax threshold.)

16. As we are trying to produce an illustrative figure we can't go into all the factors that affect the question of how rich an individual is (see Note 6 to Chapter 3 on p. 38), but it's essential to take account of the difference between single people and couples who have a single joint income as far as the Inland Revenue is concerned.

17. The figures in the Inland Revenue's *Survey of Personal Incomes 1982 – 83* can be broken down into individual incomes by assuming for these purposes that joint incomes are shared equally between

husband and wife. There were about 725,000 individual incomes (1.7 per cent of the adult population) over £15,000 on this basis in 1982/83, with all the after-tax income over the after-tax equivalent of £15,000 per head adding up to £3,109 million.

18. To this distribution we need to add a distribution of the additional taxable capacity derived from wealth. There are two conceptual difficulties here:

(i) The distribution of wealth doesn't vary consistently with income, and little is known about the overlap in ranking and personnel between the upper tails of the two distributions (see paragraph 23). In other words, we don't know how many of the top 1 per cent of earners are in the top 1 per cent of wealth holders and vice versa.

(ii) There is no strictly comparable method of taxing income and wealth, and in Britain no annual wealth tax which could relate this exercise to real life. Further, there is a political problem about "confiscating" capital that doesn't produce wealth. However, as this exercise is concerned with moral judgements rather than with practical tax systems, and it is possible to express wealth in terms of income, income and wealth shall be treated as interchangeable. (This calculation is in income terms because it is easier to express in terms of income how much money the poor need to lift them out of poverty.)

19. The income equivalent of wealth has been calculated from estimates of distribution of marketable wealth among individuals (*Inland Revenue Statistics 1985*, Series C: this doesn't include private pension rights, which are for these purposes "deferred income"). It is defined as the "annuity value" of wealth — that is, the amount of perpetual income that someone would regard as being equivalent to their capital. This depends on assumptions about capital yields, inflation, the capital tax regime and the income tax regime on the notional annuity income. Interest rates in the past three years have been generally around 10 per cent, as have earnings on shares, although share prices and house prices have risen by rather more. If we take 10 per cent as a minimised-risk return, the capital yield after inflation, averaged over 1983 – 86, was 5 per cent. Approximately this real yield could be obtained on government securities (gilts) free of tax. So I assume that an after-tax annual income of 5 per cent of capital is equivalent to that capital.

20. In addition to the information in *Inland Revenue Statistics 1985*, that the top 1.8 per cent of adults (764,000 people) in 1983 held wealth of over £100,000, the Inland Revenue has provided un-published estimates for the threshold for the top 1 and 2 per cent of adults: £145,000 and £93,000 respectively. I have interpolated the thresholds of other percentile groups, and calculated the "surplus" above the income equivalent of threshold wealth.

21. Using a spreadsheet computer program estimates have been produced of the distribution of "surplus" earned income and income from wealth for the top 3.5 per cent of income-receivers and, separately, wealth-holders. The income-receivers distribution excludes unearned income, which would otherwise be double-counted, both from the after-tax "surplus" and the before-tax earnings thresholds.

22. The income figures are updated from 1982/83 to April 1986 in line with the top decile of male net earnings (derived by the Treasury from the New Earnings Survey in a parliamentary answer to Peter Shore, 28 November 1986) and the wealth figures have been updated from calendar 1983 to April 1986 at 10 per cent per annum (approximately the prevailing interest rate on government securities).

23. Both distributions are then combined and an "overlap factor" subtracted, because the top income-receivers are not all the same people as the top wealth-owners. The evidence on the nature and extent of this overlap is discussed on p. 19. Although earnings and income from wealth are closely related, there is a lack of detailed information relating wealth holdings to income at different levels of both. I have assumed a 75 per cent overlap, that is, three-quarters of the top 1 per cent of income-receivers (including income from wealth) are in the top 1 per cent of wealth-holders, or have such high incomes as to match the income equivalent of wealth of the top 1 per cent of wealth-holders, and vice versa. Approximately 60 per cent of those who have enough earnings to be "rich" on this definition have *some* income-producing assets, according to the Survey of Personal Incomes data (which underrecord some relatively minor categories of asset such as building society accounts). Given that owner-occupied property isn't included in these figures, 75 per cent is probably an underestimate (see paragraph 26).

24. To produce a "surplus" of around £11,156 million, the amount required to eliminate poverty as estimated in paragraph 12, at 75 per cent efficiency we have to take the top 2.6 per cent as our cut-off point — the actual numbers of "the rich" are 75 per cent of this number (a quarter of those with incomes high enough to be in the top 2.6 per cent are assumed not to have enough wealth or extra income to qualify as rich, and vice versa). This is 800,000 individuals, or 2 per cent of the adult population.

25. To produce the surplus required to eliminate the lower estimate of poverty, we need to cut off the top 1.7 per cent, or 550,000 after deducting the overlap factor. The April 1986 values for the income and wealth of these cut-off points are given in paragraph 2.

26. If we increase the overlap to 85 per cent, the cut-off is the top 2.35 per cent. The number of the rich is the same — 800,000 or 2 per cent of the population — but the income and wealth threshold is then slightly higher at £15,700 and £110,000 (April 1986 values).

Critique

27. These sums don't take family structure into account beyond the second income in two-earner married couples. Nor is the Married Man's Tax Allowance taken into account, which distorts the after-tax picture as between married and single people. A more important question is whether people can be regarded as equally "rich" if they have dependent spouses or children, and whether people living together in a household need the same income to maintain the same standard of living as single people. These are areas that could be refined, but any adjustment would be arbitrary: two adults living together clearly don't need twice a single person's income to live at the same standard, but what fraction should be settled on? (See "equivalence scales", Note 6 to Chapter 3 on p. 38.) To a certain extent having children is a "consumer expense" that people — especially the rich — are free to choose to spend their money on in preference to other things. Having one parent at home and not employed is, for the rich, a similarly "free" decision. For the record, seven out of every eight tax units among "the rich" on our definition is a married couple, a large proportion of them with a wife (sic: Inland Revenue terminology) not employed, so that there is an average of 1.5 adults per (employment) income among the rich.

BIBLIOGRAPHY

Tony Atkinson, *Unequal Shares*, Allen Lane 1972.

Tony Atkinson, *The Economics of Inequality*, Oxford: Clarendon Press 1975.

Tony Atkinson, *Social Justice and Public Policy*, Brighton: Wheatsheaf Books 1982.

Tony Atkinson and Alan Harrison, *The Distribution of Personal Wealth in Britain*, Cambridge University Press 1978.

Wilfred Beckerman (ed.), *The Labour Government's Economic Record 1964–70*, Duckworth 1972.

Philip Chappell and Nigel Vinson, *Owners All*, Centre for Policy Studies 1985.

Confederation of British Industry, *Tax: Time for Change*, 1985.

Maurice Cowling, *Conservative Essays*, Cassell 1978.

Diamond Commission. *See* Royal Commission of the Distribution of Income and Wealth.

Keith Dixon, *Freedom and Equality*, Routledge and Kegan Paul 1986.

John Donaldson and Pamela Philby (eds.), *Pay Differentials*, Gower 1985.

Frank Field (ed.), *The Wealth Report*, Routledge and Kegan Paul 1979.

Frank Field (ed.), *The Wealth Report 2*, Routledge and Kegan Paul 1983.

Duncan Gallie, *Social Inequality and Class Radicalism in France and Britain*, Cambridge University Press 1983.

Anthony Giddens. *See* Philip Stanworth.

C.D. Harbury and D.M.W.N. Hitchens, *Inheritance and Wealth Inequality in Britain*, George Allen and Unwin 1979.

Alan Harrison, *The Distribution of Wealth in Ten Countries* (Royal Commission on the Distribution of Income and Wealth, Background Paper No 7), HMSO 1979.
See also Professor Tony Atkinson.

Gordon Heald and Robert J. Wybrow, *The Gallup Survey of Britain*, Croom Helm 1986.

D.M.W.N. Hitchens. *See* C.D. Harbury.

David Howell, *Blind Victory: A Study in Income, Wealth and Power*, Hamish Hamilton 1986.

Keith Joseph and J. Sumption, *Equality*, John Murray 1979.

John Kay and Mervyn King, *The British Tax System*, Oxford University Press, fourth edition, 1986.

William Kay, *Tycoons*, Piatkus 1985.

Louis Kelso, *The Capitalist Manifesto*, New York: Random House 1958.

Neil Kinnock, *The Future of Socialism*, Fabian Society 1986.

Phillip Knightley, "The Gilded Tax-Dodgers", *Sunday Times*, 5 October to 2 November 1980, later published as a book, *The Vestey Affair*, Macdonalds 1981.

Labour Party, *Labour's Programme 1982*.

Roger Lawson and Vic George (eds.), *Poverty and Inequality in Common Market Countries*, Routledge and Kegan Paul 1980.

Michael McCarthy, *Campaigning for the Poor: CPAG and the Politics of Welfare*, Croom Helm 1986.

Joanna Mack and Stewart Lansley, *Poor Britain* (based on London Weekend Television series *Breadline Britain*), George Allen and Unwin 1985.

Meacher Report ("The Structure of Personal Income Taxation and Income Support", unfinished report of a sub-committee chaired by Michael Meacher MP), Third Special Report from the House of Commons Treasury and Civil Service Committee, with Minutes of Evidence and Appendices, HMSO 1983.

John Stuart Mill, *Utilitarianism* (1863) and *On Liberty* (1859), published together, H.B. Acton (ed.), J.M. Dent (Everyman) 1972.

Robert Nisbet, *Conservatism*, Open University Press 1986.

Brian Nolan, *Recent Changes in the UK Income Distribution: the Importance of Macro-Economic Conditions*, Economic and Social Research Council programme on Taxation, Incentives and the Distribution of Income, Discussion Paper 86, June 1985.

Pamela Philby. *See* John Donaldson.

Plato, *Laws*, translated by R.G. Bury, Heinemann 1926.

John Rawls, *A Theory of Justice*, Oxford University Press 1971.

Review Body on Top Salaries, *Ninth Report on Top Salaries* (Report No 23: Cmnd. 9785), HMSO 1986.

Royal Commission on the Distribution of Income and Wealth (Diamond Commission), *Report No 5: Third report on the standing reference* (Cmnd. 6999), HMSO 1977.

Report No 6: Lower incomes (Cmnd. 7175), HMSO 1978.

See also Alan Harrison.

Walter Runciman, *Relative Deprivation and Social Justice*, Routledge and Kegan Paul 1966.

Cedric Sandford and Oliver Morrissey, *The Irish Wealth Tax*, Dublin, Economic and Social Research Institute, 1985.

Cedric Sandford, J.R.M. Willis and D.J. Ironside, *An Accessions Tax*, Institute for Fiscal Studies 1973.

Stephen Smith, *Britain's Shadow Economy*, Oxford University Press 1986.

Social Democratic Party, *Fairness and Enterprise: Tax Reform Proposals*, Green Paper No 21, October 1985.

Philip Stanworth and Anthony Giddens (eds.), *Elites and Power in British Society*, Cambridge University Press 1974.

R.H. Tawney, *Equality* (1931), George Allen and Unwin, fourth edition, 1952.

Cyril Taylor, *Employment Examined: the Right approach to more jobs*, Centre for Policy Studies 1986.

Top Salaries Review Body. *See* Review Body on Top Salaries.

Peter Townsend, *Poverty in the United Kingdom*, Penguin 1979.

Nigel Tutt, *The Tax Raiders: The Rossminster Affair*, Financial Training 1985.

Tony Vernon-Harcourt, *Top Management Remuneration*, Debden Green, Saffron Walden: Charterhouse/Monks Publications, annual.

Josiah Wedgwood, *The Economics of Inheritance*, Penguin 1939.

Robert J. Wybrow. *See* Gordon Heald.

INDEX